Serv

earn,
earni

to S

Serving to Learn, Learning to Serve

Civics and Service From A to Z

Cynthia Parsons

CORWIN PRESS, INC.
A Sage Publications Company
Thousand Oaks, California

For information address:

Corwin Press, Inc.
A Sage Publications Company
2455 Teller Road
Thousand Oaks, California 91320
E-mail: order@corwin.sagepub.com

SAGE Publications Ltd.
6 Bonhill Street
London EC2A 4PU
United Kingdom

SAGE Publications India Pvt. Ltd.
M-32 Market
Greater Kailash I
New Delhi 110 048 India

Printed in the United States of America

Library of Congress Cataloging-in-Publication Data

Parsons, Cynthia.
  Serving to learn, learning to serve: Civics and service from A to Z /
Cynthia Parsons.
    p.   cm.
  ISBN 0-8039-6364-5 (alk. paper).—ISBN 0-8039-6365-3 (pbk.:
alk. paper)
    1. Student service—United States. 2. Student volunteers in
social service—United States. 3. Civics—Study and teaching—
United States. I. Title.
  LC220.5.P36 1995
  361.3'7—dc20   95-21434

This book is printed on acid-free paper.

96 97 98 99 10 9 8 7 6 5 4 3 2 1

Corwin Press Production Editor: Tricia K. Bennett
Corwin Press Typesetter: Andrea D. Swanson

Contents

Introduction   vii

About the Author   xv

A Is for Awards and Appreciation   1

B Is for Books and Birthdays   5

C Is for Civics, Civility, and Concern   7

D Is for Daring and Doing   11

E Is for Equity   15

F Is for French (and Other Foreign Languages)   19

G Is for Government   23

H Is for Helping   29

I Is for Interns   35

J Is for Justice   37

K Is for Kindness   41

L Is for Like What? and Liability   46

M Is for Money   51

N Is for Natural Science   54

O Is for Obligation   57

P Is for Physical Education   59

Q Is for Quid pro Quo   61

R Is for Recreation   65

S Is for SerVermont   68

T Is for Time and Transportation   71

U Is for the United States of America   75

V Is for Value   78

W Is for Who   80

X Is for Xenophilia   83

Y Is for Youth   86

Z Is for Zeal   89

Useful Resources: Books and Reports   91

Introduction

Howard Swearer, while president of Brown University, stated that it was his view that "participation by students in volunteer activities that are important to the community is one way of both enhancing education and developing a sense of civic pride and values." This view is my view for school children as well as for college students.

Just doing some service in the community doesn't automatically enhance academic course work, nor does participation in the solving of a civic need automatically develop a sense of civic pride and morally sound values in the doer. We teachers have to work at making the positive connection between civic service and the study of civics.

But sad to say, it would appear that more school- and college-age youths today are required to do community service as a punishment—drummed into them as something owed back to the community—than are doing service voluntarily, expecting to improve academic skills through hands-on work and learning how to become valued members of the community through service to the nonprofit sector.

Every decade or so, popular educators talk up "learning by doing," often citing John Dewey as their authority for espousing such a method of learning for school children. Unfortunately, learning *by* doing is often reduced to learning *and* doing. This is particularly true with student community service. Too often pupils carry out a service—seen by their teachers as primarily good for character building—and do their school lessons quite separately from the service activities.

I don't mean to take anything away from the enormously important personal lessons school students learn by engaging in service activities and helping to solve or alleviate serious community needs. But what's enormously exciting is the fact that intrinsic to every service project are academically related learning-by-doing possibilities. That's why this book was written and why there are more than 100 suggestions of ways to integrate course work (K-12) with service work. Adele Simmons, president of the MacArthur Foundation, has stated that "public service is a way to connect educational values with community action in a reciprocal relationship." She elaborates on the connection between such service and the need for the schools to teach the basics of democracy to all students.

"Important links," she asserts, "can be forged between students and society much to the advantage of both. Students are exposed to real life situations and conditions of human need, and the community gains dedicated, well-educated volunteers."

Making those links between students and society is today—and always has been—the fundamental work of our public schools. It's from school lessons and interrelated community service activities that our children learn how to be small "d" democrats.

Teachers who provide relevant reading and research assignments linked to volunteer work activity, hold individual and group discussions based on what students have learned while doing service work, assign papers that describe and analyze service experiences, encourage the keeping of private journals linking what's learned through service with what's taught in the classroom, and use civic experience to enhance the academic study of civics are carrying out an essential part of their public mandate.

We need to fuse (i.e., to link) book learning with practical experience—most particularly with involvement in making sure that the "pursuit of happiness" is not for some privileged few but for each and every member of our community.

In 1939, on the eve of World War II, Edward Benes, then president of Czechoslovakia, wrote in his famous book, *Democracy Today and Tomorrow*, "Democracy is a benefit always in danger and always to be defended." He elaborated, "A democratic regime means agreement, evolution, cooperation. Democracy must respect truth, honesty, fair play, and individual freedom." Of totalitarianism he noted that it counts on "hate, intolerance, blind partisanship, mystical prejudices, and fanatical faith."

These tyrannical traits he would replace with such moral and spiritual qualities as "reason, moderation, mutual respect, tolerance, education, and good will." Where better for our children to develop these moral characteristics than while serving alongside the most spiritually minded adults in their community?

Our schools must teach children not only the *rights* stemming from our democratic way of life but also the *responsibilities*. To understand the system of justice in our democracy, for example, our youngsters need to be observers and sometime volunteer workers in courtrooms, public defender offices, detention centers, and police departments. We cannot remove our children for 12 (or 16) years from the workplaces of democracy in our communities and expect them to know how to be responsible participatory small "d" democrats just from having read about and passed tests on U.S. citizenship in school classrooms.

Schuyler M. Meyer, Jr., while president of the Edwin Gould Foundation for Children, stated in the booklet, *Making Small "d" Democrats*,

> We are convinced that caring community service is a strong antidote to greed, selfishness, and fragmentation in our public and private institutions. Community service is both liberating and instructive.
>
> Serving is so important as an aid to help each child mature; is so vital to the well being of democratic communities; is so essential to further the causes of social justice—that every young person should be engaged in service.
>
> Starting very early, service should be incorporated into every learning environment.... When a 5th grade class "adopts" a nursing home; kindergartners fold napkins for a local

hospital; the special education industrial arts class repairs household appliances for handicapped neighbors, democracy is being learned and expressed. This is a vital way for young people to learn how to form "a more perfect union"; that is, to learn how to become small "d" democrats. (pp. 1, 3-4)

In other words, community service provides a laboratory experience for students engaged in the study of citizenship in the United States. Alexis de Tocqueville, a French statesman who visited the United States in 1831 to study our emerging democracy, wrote compellingly about linking service and study:

It cannot be doubted in the United States the instruction of the people powerfully contributes to the support of the democratic republic; and such must always be the case, I believe, where the instruction which enlightens the understanding is not separated from the moral education which amends the heart.

But I would not exaggerate this advantage, and I am still further from thinking, as so many people do think in Europe, that men can be instantaneously made citizens by teaching themselves to read and write.

True information is mainly derived from experience; and if the Americans had not been gradually accustomed to govern themselves, their book-learning would not help them much at the present day. (Kershner, 1983)

In 1831, as de Tocqueville noted, the United States was the "only country on the face of the earth where the citizens enjoy unlimited freedom of association for political purposes" (Kershner, 1983). That's no longer true; today, many nations have embraced both representative and participatory democracy. But we were the first; we are the leaders and the world's teachers.

Sad to say, just as we've not taught all our school children to read and write (nationwide our public schools register a 30% rate of failure), we've not taught our youths the importance of casting votes in local, state, and national elections (the failure rate here is close to 70%).

Every high school needs to send a letter to every 18-year-old that is similar to the one used by the Somerville (Massachusetts) High School, which I quote here with permission:

> Dear _____:
> Congratulations on turning 18! This is an especially significant milestone for you. It means that you are now an official ADULT with the right to help decide how things should be run. Adulthood means being entitled to certain rights and privileges. It also means assuming more responsibility for yourself and your community.
> Perhaps the most important right to which you are now entitled is the right to VOTE. Look around our town. Does the government do enough for you? Are you happy with the way things are run? The schools? Police and Fire Departments? Parks and Playgrounds? Do you think your family's rent [or property tax] is too high? Do you think you should be paid less than minimum wage just because you are under age 20?
> Unless you vote, you allow other people to make these decisions for you.
> You may register to vote at the Election Department in the City Hall or right here at school.
> Sincerely yours,

In one small Vermont town, where very few school students do any service-learning activities and there's next to no recognition of the 18-year-old milestone linked to participatory democracy, the voter checklist in 1990 showed 1,737 eligible voters, yet only 371 citizens actually marked a ballot in an important election that year. Although we know that 21% of those over age 18 voted, what we don't know, because no exit poll was taken, was precisely how many of those who voted were between the ages of 18 and 25.

An informal survey of the checklist revealed that almost no one in that age bracket had voted. One clear test of whether service learning is making a difference for school children would be for each secondary school to monitor the checklist for each election, noting the rise or fall in participation of voting-age students as well as recent dropouts and graduates. Are those young adults (18- to 25-year-olds) whose civics course is (was) linked with some community service more or less inclined to vote than those citizens who are (were) given no service-learning opportunities while in school?

If a school district made a serious effort to celebrate the coming of age of its 18-year-old voters, offered all students at least one course that integrated civics instruction with some civic service, and engaged all pupils (K-12) in service-learning activities throughout the community, isn't it safe to surmise that nearly all of its students who were eligible to vote would do so?

Isn't it correct to state that this school district is carrying out its mandate to make small "d" democrats better than a school district that provides students with little or no civic service linked with civics instruction and undertakes no celebration of the right to vote?

Voting, of course, is not the only responsibility our young people need to understand and practice in a democracy based on "the people" as sovereign. Many community problems require the direct attention of responsible citizens. A fifth grader explained to me why he was serving on a task force to get a school budget passed: "If we didn't have enough money, we'd have to stop going on school buses every week to the senior center, and that wouldn't be fair. They would miss us, and we wouldn't get to practice reading aloud to the ones who can't read for themselves."

There are considerable mathematical skills to be learned studying a school budget and strong language arts lessons involved in oral reading. But more, there are important lessons in caring, sharing, consideration, patience, tolerance, and selflessness.

This fifth grader knew about those. He and the rest of his class had written a song about the preservation of a rain forest, had learned to sign (for the deaf) their song, and had performed it for hard-of-hearing adults and children. When I tried to say that the signing was something special, he disagreed: "That's the way some people hear, and it wouldn't be fair for us to sing it to them, and them not hear it."

Dennis Thayer, principal of Thayer High School in Winchester, New Hampshire, asserts that what goes on in most schools "is teacher talk and student passivity." Not so at his public high school. There, he explains,

We talk about the student as worker. I judge a class not by how dynamic the teacher is, but by the outcomes for the students. The main thing we're trying to do at Thayer is to engage students in an intellectual way. Students are learning science, not when they are doing a book assignment, but when they are studying plant communities to make a wilderness trail or trying to figure out why a river is polluted.

His ideal class? "When kids in a group or individually are working on a problem, trying to solve something." This book is written for such creative individuals: children, adolescents, teachers, and mentors.

From A to Z, what does service learning do?

- Helps students learn
- Enriches the curriculum
- Produces alert, helpful, and voting citizens
- Brings schools, families, and communities together
- Enlivens the meaning of democracy
- Recasts the roles of students and schools
- Stimulates teachers to put course work in context
- Protects and encourages active, experiential teaching
- Teaches the usefulness and relevance of the 3 Rs
- Prepares students for full-time work assignments
- Ensures that young doers will be lifetime doers
- Shows why giving is getting

About the Author

Cynthia Parsons coordinates a statewide service-learning initiative known as SerVermont. She is the author of two other books on education: *Seeds*, dealing with school reform issues, and *The Co-op Bridge*, exploring work-study and cooperative education programs for middle and high school students. Beginning in 1948, she taught in both private and public schools in California, Vermont, Massachusetts, and New York. Subsequently, she made a career change to journalism and, for 14 years, was the education editor of the *Christian Science Monitor*. Her undergraduate degree in education is from Principia College; her master's in education is from Antioch/ Putney; and in 1985, she received an honorary doctorate from Norwich University. She has taught—using service learning—at every grade level, including visiting instructorships at Syracuse University, Dartmouth, the University of Vermont, and Tufts. She has received many honors and awards for her writing and for her volunteer service activities, but she is particularly proud of the eagle feather (carved out of glass) given to her by the National Indian Youth Leadership program and of the Eleanor Roosevelt Public Service medal she received in honor of her work in national service and service learning.

A Is for Awards and Appreciation

CITIZENS: MADE NOT BORN

The bell has tolled for communism. But its concrete construction has not yet collapsed. It might happen that instead of liberation, we will find ourselves buried under its ruins.

Neglected by family and school, our youth is growing if not toward crime then toward a thoughtless barbaric imitation of something luring them from abroad.

The historical Iron Curtain perfectly defended our country from all things good in the West—from civil freedom, respect of personality, diversity of personal activity, overall well-being, charity movements. But that Curtain was incomplete, letting in through a gap the manure of degraded pop, mass culture, vulgar fashions, and the lowest refuse of publicity. This rubbish was greedily soaked up by our deprived youth.

Russia does need democracy and needs it badly, but given the complete unpreparedness of our people for complicated democratic life, it should be gradually, patiently, and solidly built from the bottom up, and not just proclaimed by mass media and introduced from above in a torrent, all at once, in its entirety.

—Alexander Solzhenitsyn

Awards for Student Volunteers

Parents. You could establish a student community service award for those youngsters who respond to a community need, possibly during an emergency. For example, an elementary school youngster who lived next door to a blind couple, seeing smoke coming from their kitchen window, entered their trailer home, led them both to safety, and then called the fire department. He was cited during a school assembly and at a PTA meeting.

Managers of Government and Nonprofit Agencies. You could band together to provide awards to students whose volunteer efforts have been particularly useful. For example, the manager of a hospital asked patients to list those student volunteers they thought deserving and posted their names on a bulletin board in the Visitors' Center.

School Personnel. At the very least you could see to it that school announcements include special achievements by student volunteers. You could maintain a special bulletin board on which such citations are posted. You could call parents to tell them of some honor being given their child for exemplary student community service.

At commencement exercises or awards ceremonies, a special award could be reserved for the student volunteer(s), chosen by all the students by secret ballot. It could be given to a class group, such as the environmental science class that planted a new strain of elm trees; to a pair of students; or to a single student. The school superintendent, asking for secret ballot votes from students and staff at each school, could give a community service award to someone at each school during National Volunteer Week.

The governor could ask a commission to set up criteria for Governor's Awards for Volunteer Activity, reserving one award for a high school student and another for a college student, with nominations to come from those for whom the service was done. This has actually been done in Vermont.

A personal note: During a severe storm, my mother's car was swept into 10 feet of saltwater off a boat-launching ramp, causing all electrical systems to short. A passerby stopped his car and organized her rescue, quickly shedding his pants and shoes to enter the water. He was asked to come to the next city council meeting to receive a citation, which he did, taking my mother with him. He said he really didn't care about the award, that saving a life was reward enough. But for my mother it was very important. And for the city? It was the first such rescue from that dangerous area; all other victims swept down the ramp had been lost. Now that access to the water has been rerouted and blocked off during storms.

Another personal note: I have served for several years on the Hitachi Foundation's review board for the Yoshiama Awards for outstanding service by high school seniors. Each year there are more nominees; each year the quality of the service performed by the finalists has improved dramatically; each year the students find the award and the recognition a spur to thinking of more and more effective ways to serve.

Awards From Student Volunteers

During each marking period, elementary school students within each neighborhood might choose a community person to honor who has "made a difference."

1. Write letters of appreciation to them.
2. Do a class book about what the person did and give it to the local library.
3. Write and give radio announcements about the award during public service time.
4. Prepare a cable television appreciation message.
5. In social studies class, learn about others who have been given special awards for helping a community and making a difference.
6. Invite the award winner to school and give "three cheers" at lunch.

Middle school and high school students could do all that has been suggested for the elementary students; in addition, they could look for members of the community who should receive awards for their contributions to technology, health, or the arts. The award could be made by the whole school or some particular group of students. Funds could be raised for the favorite charity of the award winner.

In sum, awards and appreciation are not only ways of recognizing the deserving but also ways of showing students how important it is for each to help and support the other—how that improves the civility in civics, eschews servitude, and enhances service.

Celebrations

A smile is a celebration. Many students tell me that all they wish for when they help someone in need is to see the person smile. That, they explain, is the only award they want. We teachers need to become better celebrators; we're much too accustomed to greeting each effort by a student with a critique, a pointing out of what could have been better. Instead, we need to observe, commemorate, and praise both the service activities and the related academic growth. We need to learn how to celebrate each individual's growth and avoid odious comparisons or the placing of students on some arbitrary curve of assumed effort and ability.

B Is for Books and Birthdays

CITIZENS: MADE NOT BORN

It is not only the quantitative growth of active programs and of interest in service learning, but also the growing understanding of the significant role that involvement in community service can play for all young people that prompts us to believe that we are entering a new era: of links between schools and communities, and of opportunities for young people to become active learners and contributors in their schools and communities.

—Joan Schine

First, Books

For every non-English-speaking preschooler, prepare alphabet and number books in both English and the preschooler's own language; have the books focus on community service centers and significant buildings. Invite interested community members to read the books and come to school for a discussion period. Ask that teams of students, each including a community member, do a short skit based on one scene in the book. Every computer student could either be tutored by an adult computer specialist from the community or himself tutor a beginner. A computer class or group of computer students might rewrite a popular program to be more user friendly for learners with special needs. Every upper-grade student could offer to read to and be read to by a lower-grade pupil on a regular basis. Students might perform the research and do all graphs and artwork for reports needed by town officials regarding water, sewage, zoning, recycling, recreation, and so on.

A student might team up with a college student and work with one community adult who has not yet learned to read and write fluently. As the adult pupil begins to learn, either write or provide books at the appropriate reading level.

Be a storyteller at your public library.

Second, Birthdays

Sometime in September, invite everyone in the community who had an 85th (or higher) birthday since the previous May to come to school for lunch with special cake made by student cooks. Sing a medley of songs to all birthday celebrants and send them away with surprise gifts made in arts or crafts.

Each marking period, through churches, visiting nurses, local police, and the like, locate all citizens in the community aged 85 or older living alone, and around the time of each person's birthday, start a pen pal or phone pal relationship. Through an appropriate agency, learn what artwork might be appreciated, whether talking books would be appropriate, and if the elderly persons are mobile, whether they have a way to get to school for a meal, some songs, and a play.

Note: Joan Braun, the community service coordinator for a large rural high school, received a cake from the home economics teacher that had been baked as a class assignment to give to nursing home residents. She sent it back, saying, "We don't give cakes; we give kids and cakes." Fortunately, a near crisis was averted. The student bakers were more than delighted to go along with their prize work, share in the giving, and return to school refreshed and happy; the home economics teacher caught on to why kids and cakes were better than cakes alone.

C Is for Civics, Civility, and Concern

CITIZENS: MADE NOT BORN

If we wish to be free—if we mean to preserve those privileges for which we have been fighting so long—if we do not mean to abandon the noble struggle in which we have so long been engaged—we must fight! I repeat it, we must fight!

They tell us that we are weak, unable to deal with so powerful an enemy. But when shall we be stronger?

We are not weak if we make proper use of the means which the God of nature has granted us. Three million people, armed in the holy cause of liberty, and in such a country as ours, cannot be conquered by any force which our enemy can send against us.

The battle is not won by the strong alone. It is won by the alert, the active, the brave.

—Patrick Henry, c. 1775

One summer, I hired two interns to search out all possible service-learning jobs available in one Vermont county. One intern was a college student on an independent-study project earning course credits from the sociology department; the other was a junior high student earning some back-to-school clothes money, whose task it was to take notes during interviews and help with organization of the data collected.

I was eager to find out—particularly from government and non-profit agencies who used adult volunteers but had never used student volunteers—(a) whether they ever would and (b) why they never had.

The interns received a warm welcome from private nonprofit organizations, particularly those where confidentiality was not a concern. They were made unwelcome by most government agencies—federal, state, and local.

Typical was the response of the local game warden. He called me to ask, "Just what is this all about? I have no use for students. They belong in school."

After explaining the interns' task and why they were going to every nonprofit office in the county, I then remarked that, "The Gophers of Minnesota must be getting ahead of the Woodchucks of Vermont, as the game wardens in that state have youths help them man their hotline." There was a short pause, then over the phone came, "Hmmm, good idea."

That remark—"They [the students] belong in school"—is a common refrain from town officials. Yet some of the most meaningful learning experiences come when town and gown cooperate and the children in the community feel as much a part of the community as those holding the highest offices.

In fact, in most communities the nonprofit businesses and local chambers of commerce are doing more to help students integrate academics with practical skill development than are town officials. Businesses want better trained workers; hence, they see a direct connection between how well the children in a community are schooled and the quality of their workforce. And they make room for students; they cooperate with school authorities.

That connection between how well the children in a community are schooled and the quality of their civic involvement is, I would argue, very much the business of all civil authorities. Consider the following possibilities.

For the Fire Department

- In rural areas, let students take turns being part of the local volunteer rescue and fire squad.
- In urban areas, develop a corps of fire department cadets who learn to inspect buildings and issue reports on findings.
- Let students learn to write and record public service announcements about fire safety.
- Assist in providing lessons in fire safety to younger children.
- Assist in preparation of department reports with data collection through the use of polling techniques.
- Assist in preparation of department reports by entering data onto computers or designing graphs or providing artwork.
- Translate essential material for the non-English speaking.

For the Police Department

- Let students take turns being police cadets and helping with traffic control, maintenance of safety codes, and teaching lessons in safety for younger pupils.
- Assist the police community relations department with drug, alcohol, and vandalism concerns.
- Provide, under police department guidance, an escort service for the elderly and handicapped.
- Provide drivers for the legally drunk.
- Monitor police band radio, doing a periodic statistical analysis of police concerns.
- Integrate all school-related drug and alcohol education with police department concerns, procedures, and policies.
- Assist with all public relations efforts; prepare material for cable TV on police concerns; prepare police bulletins for radio public school announcement (PSA) time.
- "Adopt" a precinct and learn how to organize a community crime watch.
- Translate essential material for the non-English speaking.

For the Town Clerk and Business Manager

- File
- Type
- Stuff envelopes
- Answer the phone
- Use the copy machine
- Use the calculator
- Enter computer data
- Write memos and reports
- Design graphs
- Collate data
- Analyze data
- Research files
- Translate
- Run errands
- Be a "gofer"
- Water the plants
- Do light maintenance

For the Town Treasurer. As in the other town departments, pupils can help with filing, copying, sorting, stuffing envelopes, telephoning, taking messages, and other office chores. But older students might take on more serious work. They might develop graphs and charts for use at public meetings or in published reports. They might carry out analyses of incomes and expenditures for selected public concerns, such as water, sewer, road maintenance, street cleaning, and so forth. Certainly those in computer classes could practice their new data processing skills while aiding the treasurer's office.

D Is for Daring and Doing

CITIZENS: MADE NOT BORN

If the young were born literate, there would be no need to teach them literature; if they were born citizens, there would be no need to teach them civic responsibility.

—Benjamin R. Barber

Doing

As I've stated previously, the United States of America isn't just a representative democracy; it's a participatory democracy. Learning to serve our communities—for the good of all—is one of the most rewarding school lessons. It's this service that undergirds what the United States stands for. There's our bumper sticker slogan again: Serving to learn; learning to serve.

Infants learn to walk and run by walking and running. They learn to talk by talking. Children learn to sing by singing. They learn to play ball by playing with a ball. Youths learn to use a computer by using a computer, to type by typing, to use the scientific method by using the scientific method, and to appreciate great literature by reading it.

But let's take that *doing* a step further. A skilled coach generally improves your game more than any amount of individual trial and error. The same with great literature: It's all well and good to read it on one's own, but how much more meaningful to be able to discuss nuances with a serious scholar. And how much more fruitful it might be to carry out scientific experiments guided by a competent scientist.

All of which is a preface to my argument that sending students out into the community to do X hours of service and considering that a good way to teach democracy, is no more rational than to put a child in the deep end of the pool to see whether he or she can swim. Or no more responsible than turning over the science lab for an hour a week to students to "do something" without guidance, reflective thought, and evaluation.

What kind of educator or school board member would consider he or she was providing an adequate education for a community's children if no community service was undertaken during 12 or 13 years of schooling? What is going on in the head of a principal of a school with some 350 to 1,000 students who thinks it sufficient that the bells ring on time and the students move from classroom to classroom, 6 hours a day for 180 days, doing little more than reading, reciting, listening, writing, and taking tests? How can he or she rest content if no pupil in the building ever tutors another pupil? Never cooperates with a group of students to solve a community problem? Never looks at any portion of the town budget during the last 5 years of math? Never contributes one word to a community agency news-letter? Never prepares a public service announcement for a nonprofit agency in the community? What kind of educator would consider it unnecessary to provide "doing" experiences to complement seat work?

Daring

When I talk with youngsters about community service, service learning, and national service, I often ask the following question:

"Have you ever done something very special for someone—or possibly for a cause or organization—that no one but you and the one you did it for knew about?" I generally emphasize, "I mean done something that needed doing and really helped someone or fixed something really important, but it is so special and precious to you that you've not told anyone about it. You don't boast about it. But you feel it made a big difference in your life." I get many nodding heads; if I ask for hands, even then, though heads are willing to nod or eyes to sparkle, only a few want to raise their hands. Yes, they have done something for someone. They know what it has meant to them to make a difference.

I watched a lad one day climb up a pile of dirty, frozen snow and, using a heavy ax, break away enough ice to reveal a directional sign. I asked him, "Who sent you to do that on this cold day?"

"I told myself," he answered. "People coming into town need to know to take the next left turn if they want to stay on this road."

Was he practicing civics? Think what an alert teacher could do with that act to bring home civics lessons regarding the "common welfare" and "pursuit of happiness."

I believe it is daring, not to mandate community service, but to *dare* yourself—particularly if you are an educator—to make your school such a caring environment that volunteering and solving community needs are second nature to the pupils and integrating service and course work is second nature to the faculty.

I think it's more daring—and more pedagogically correct—to have students describe important service activities and place this description in a portfolio of achievements than to give a grade for service or to put a check mark on a report card, signifying service done.

I think it's more daring to ask that students keep a journal about service work, and no teacher ever looks at it—letting the students relish its privacy—than to have such a journal handed in, corrected, and graded.

It takes considerable daring for politicians to espouse anything to do with schooling that doesn't appear to them to have an immediate effect on raising standardized test scores and lowering dropout rates, vandalism, and drug abuse. Similarly, those whose jobs are dependent on political considerations consider it dangerous to put resources into programs that cannot be scored quantitatively.

Dare to do it; dare to involve every pupil in some community improvement project; dare to challenge every teacher to fuse service and learning; dare to involve every nonprofit private or public agency with all the public school children in the area. Dare to be a doer.

E Is for Equity

CITIZENS: MADE NOT BORN

Real government is very hard. It's probably the hardest thing humans do other than fight a civil war. The Founding Fathers spent 35 years between the Albany Congress and swearing in George Washington. They were frustrated. They were often lonely. They were defeated on occasion, and they had to keep going. They wrote long documents like The Federalist Papers *and they wrote short documents like a one-page handout, and it wasn't easy. And all too often, I hear so-called reformers come in and basically say, "I'm available for 25 minutes next Tuesday to change the world. Why don't you listen and let's have a nice dialogue?" The world doesn't work like that. People who want to change it have to buckle down and master the process of self-government; and the first rule is, it's very hard work.*

—Newt Gingrich

Establishing a participatory democracy and granting full citizenship rights to all those born in the United States continues to be a serious challenge.

- Was our country a democracy before we provided free public schooling for all children?
- Was our country a democracy when it sanctioned slavery?
- Was our country a democracy when we made gender (male) a condition for voting?
- Was our country a democracy when a citizen had to pay money to vote?
- Are we a truly representative democracy if fewer than 50% of our citizens vote?
- Are we a participatory democracy if, year after year, more than 25% of our 18-year-old youths cannot pass basic literacy tests?

As a nation, we've made some interesting decisions regarding equity and children. It was not until the 1954 Supreme Court decision outlawing separate schools based on race that most school districts with a minority population of more than 20% gave any thought to treating all pupils fairly and impartially. But the mandated changes in school equity did not take place overnight or within a year or two or three or . . .

It wasn't until a decade or two later that many school districts made a serious effort to provide equity to all races, colors, and creeds.

It wasn't just that children of different colors were educated in different buildings but that the teachers were different, the physical conditions of the buildings were different, the equipment was different, the playgrounds were different, the support services were different, the amount of money spent per pupil was different, the ratio of pupils to classroom teachers was different, the test results were different, the percentage of those accepted into 4-year colleges was different, and the percentage who dropped out before completing Grade 12 was different.

I remember being taken to an inner-city school, in the early 1960s, that had once housed only black children from the local neighborhood but was now a Grade 6 center to which white and black pupils were bused from other parts of the school district. The white sixth graders discovered that this school, unlike the ones they had attended previously, had no library, no playground, no stage, and no music room, and had not been painted inside or out for more than 25 years.

There is no way we can teach "that all men are created equal," or that they have "certain unalienable rights," such as "life, liberty and the pursuit of happiness," if we do not help our children address all questions of fairness and justice.

Take the matter of whom most schools will permit or mandate to do community service. If I were to ask educators in Prague, Sofia, Dresden, Budapest, Moscow, and Warsaw the question, "Who do you think gets to do community service in the majority of U.S. public schools?" they would probably answer, "Any student who wishes to." Unfortunately, too often that is not the case. Students in honor societies are required to do some form of outside community service; students being punished for a school infraction are often given X hours of community service as part of their punishment.

For the students with high grades or in student leadership positions, service partakes more of Kipling's "white man's burden," or government by oligarchy, than of government by, for, and of the people.

For those being punished, the purpose of service too often is not citizenship in action but servitude. For example, in Pine Bluff, Arkansas, youths under the age of 20, and some as young as 8, are ordered by the court to pick up roadway litter two Saturday mornings a month for X months as punishment for offenses such as vandalism and breaking and entering. The South Carolina Department of Parole and Community Connections states that their mandated public service program, which includes litter pickups, "promotes a work-ethic approach to punishment."

Of course, some schools do offer community service to any interested student, and a subset of these schools makes an effort to integrate the service with academic course work.

Yet service work develops good work habits even if the work itself doesn't enhance a skill. The members of a work crew that rakes leaves or shovels snow or digs trenches to divert water (or even picks up litter) might not develop any specific business skills but might learn punctuality, consistency, perseverance, and comradeship. It shouldn't take either special privilege or punishment to be given an opportunity to gain those sterling qualities. Equity demands similar lessons for all students.

As a member of the faculty of a boarding school, I was assigned the task of supervising the Saturday morning service program for "offenders"—that is, for those students who had "earned" demerits during the week. Each demerit earned a quarter hour of service work. Because I was determined that service should be recognized as a way to learn citizenship, I made the activities as rewarding (and fun) as possible so that students without demerits would volunteer. I started by asking the students to find out what the community most needed to make it a fair and just place to live.

Thus, we did chores for single elderly people; we cultivated and harvested flowers to give to shut-ins; we cultivated and harvested fruits and vegetables for the school kitchen and some hungry families in the community; we maintained two public nature trails; we carried out rescue missions on high-country trails in a primitive wilderness area; we responded to calls from the fire tower to douse smoldering campfires in mountain meadows; and we tutored, tutored, tutored.

F Is for French
(and Other Foreign Languages)

CITIZENS: MADE NOT BORN

Year	U.S. Population	Slave Population	Percentage
1790	4 million	700,000	17.5%
1810	7.2 million	1.2 million	16.6
1830	13 million	2 million	15.4
1850	23.2 million	3.2 million	14.3
1860	31.5 million	4 million	12.7
1870	40 million	0	0

I say to you today, my friends, that in spite of the difficulties and frustrations of the moment I still have a dream. It is a dream deeply rooted in the American dream. I have a dream that one day this nation will rise up and live out the true meaning of its creed: "We hold these truths to be self-evident; that all men are created equal."

—Martin Luther King, Jr., 1963

The Welcome Wagon is a business approach to a community need. When new families move into town, the business community greets them with a basket of goods and information about where they might shop. It would be wonderful if, every time a new student for whom English is a second language enters the school system, he or she could be treated to a "welcome basket" of goods and information, not only about the school and its activities but also about what's available for youths in the community. It would be particularly helpful if the written (or taped) material in the basket could be in two languages: English and the student's own.

Let's say a newly arrived family from Southeast Asia has children in Grades 1, 6, and 11. A team of primary school pupils could be responsible for providing a map of how to get from the Grade 1 room to the lunchroom, a map showing where the playground is, a "welcome to our school" card, and names and pictures of the rest of the children in the Grade 1 homeroom. Older students could help by providing a school calendar as well as information on regulations in both English and the language of the family. For the 6th and 11th graders, the basket of materials should provide information to meet their special needs.

For the adults in the family, a welcome basket of translated information about community services (police, fire, recreation, etc.) could be assembled and dispatched (or delivered) by a team of students.

All school notices being sent home could be translated by teams of students into the family's language, including information about school closings, special school events, parent nights, and so forth. In addition, pairs of students, learning a second language, could offer to help with translation for teacher-parent conferences.

The children in a primary school came predominantly from three different cultures. A good many were Chinese; many more were Hispanic; the remainder were English-speaking grandchildren of immigrants from central Europe. For a community service project, the Chinese children, together with a Chinese service organization, took all the children on a tour of a Chinese neighborhood, and together the pupils and their parents served and explained a Chinese meal in the school cafeteria. The following month the Hispanic children led a tour of their neighborhood and prepared and served a Hispanic meal. The aftermath was a continuing offer by the pupils to help out in the Chinese and Hispanic day care centers, regularly making artwork, storybooks, and plays to share.

Every child needs to know where to go for help when hungry, when abused, and when left alone with no appropriate supervision and where to find phone numbers of organizations that can protect and provide care. For example, the teenagers in one school made a booklet with this information for every child in their county, a rural one where there were many children living in isolated trailers. Teens in another school compiled such information for an urban setting, got it printed on a bookmark, which was distributed through schools and stores. The same information should be made available in every language used in non-English-speaking homes.

Is the French (or other language) class going to watch a specially ordered film? Won't they invite anyone in the immediate community interested in watching? Is the French (or other language) class going on a field trip to view French art, visit a French-speaking community, hear French music? Won't they offer to include anyone in the immediate community interested in going?

Aren't older students regularly providing the school and public library with original stories in two languages, English on the left page, second language on the right? As a part of their course work, aren't students fluent in a second language preparing lessons for beginning students of French (or other language) for cable television public service time?

I received a letter written in French and was not sure of the full meaning. Interestingly, my first thought was to ask an adult friend who had grown up in a French-speaking home some 40 years earlier. She helped me, enlisting the aid of an adult who had lived more recently in a French-speaking community. None of the three of us even gave a moment's thought to asking the school's French class, or a student in it, to help with the translation. Why?

I suppose it was because we had never heard of the language classes at the school ever performing any service for the community; we only had been asked repeatedly to give money to them so that they could travel abroad. Consider how much more willing we would have been to give generously so our community's children could study and travel abroad if we thought they were doing so to enrich our community.

In Sacramento, California, there is a waiting room at the county courthouse for witnesses as well as defendants and plaintiffs. In an adjoining children's waiting room, called La Casita, student and adult volunteers take care of little ones who must wait while their parents are in the courtroom. Spanish is the second language most needed in this room. What a wonderful place for language students not only to place books and tapes translated into Spanish, posters in two languages, and toys and games that use two languages but also to spend some time there playing and talking and listening to the little ones.

G Is for Government

CITIZENS: MADE NOT BORN

We have learned from much of our research that, in effective classrooms, young people are moved to choose to learn. When they take their own initiatives and when they care about what they are doing, they are likely to go in search of meanings, to begin learning to learn. We understand also that they are most likely to pose the questions with which learning begins when they feel themselves speaking to others, speaking in the first person to those who are different from themselves. When they can articulate what they have to say against the background of their own biographies, they may well be in a position to listen to others—and be listened to—if those others are also speaking for themselves.

—Maxine Green

Students: "In Order to Form a More Perfect Union"

- Organize and conduct voter registration drives.
- Assist with completing absentee ballots by those unable to write.

- Staff a baby-sitting and infant care center at or near a polling place.
- Assist with handicapped and elderly at voting booths.
- Track and publish the voting records of all elected officials serving your community.
- Provide advocate service for any persons in the community experiencing racial, religious, or economic discrimination.
- Regularly provide opinion columns on community issues for the op-ed pages of local newspapers.
- Regularly provide editorials for public service time on radio and television.
- Form a committee structure at school for research and discussion on issues affecting the school community.
- Serve on school decision-making committees.
- Combine service with governance concerns.

As an example of this last suggestion, Joe Nathan, author of *Free to Teach*, taught an elective course in a St. Paul, Minnesota, school called Consumer Rights and Responsibilities. The purpose was not only to teach the students about consumer needs but to do so through community service advocacy. His class advertised in the local media, offering assistance to those in the community with consumer grievances. One person called with a case involving an alleged consumer violation by a local car dealership. The customer claimed that the radio she was promised was not in the car when delivered and that the dealer had refused to make restitution.

Before deciding whether to take this particular case, the students talked it over, finally deciding to do so and agreeing as a class which team of students would take the case and what should be the first steps.

The car owner received the following letter from the class, composed by the team and written by one of them: "Your case was brought up in our class, and we have agreed to work on it. We have discussed it and we would like a copy of your contract. From there we will write to you and tell you our next step. Sincerely yours, [signed] Consumer Action Service Students." After the contract arrived, the students and teacher discussed possible next steps, and three students acted out a possible scenario with one student calling the dealership to talk with the owner.

To help the students, Joe Nathan invited officials from the Better Business Bureau and the Consumer Protection Agency, a public interest research group, to come and talk with the class, provide reading material, and act as consultants for the cases they took on.

The students applied their research well; the client got her radio. In fact, this class resolved satisfactorily for their clients more than 50% of all the cases they took on. But best of all, they learned an important way "to form a more perfect union."

Students: "Establish Justice"

- Run errands for court clerks and court-appointed lawyers.
- Be a phone pal of, hence part of the support team for, a youth on probation.
- Include youths on probation when doing group community service, such as park cleanup, rehabilitation of a homeless shelter, soup kitchen food preparation, celebratory meals for elderly in the community, or caroling at nursing homes.
- Serve on school juries deciding guilt or innocence and determining punishment for proven offenses.
- Serve on school arbitration panels.
- Serve on out-of-school youth arbitration panels.

Ask any student in any school who the *best* teacher in the school is. After you get your answer, ask why the student named that particular teacher, and you will hear the word *fair*. I met a fellow older adult, now a retired lawyer, and in our brief autobiographical exchanges I learned the name of the public high school she'd attended. I grinned and said, "Then you surely had Miss H_____ for math."

"I did, I did. What a tyrant." Then this lawyer, thinking back some 40 years, asserted, "Fair. She was fair. She was tough. If she hadn't been fair, we'd have probably drowned her in the river!"

There was a pause, then she said, "My gosh. Talk about community service. She made us all find some instance of the use of mathematics by town government that we could improve on—and we did."

In the 1990 electoral race for governor of Vermont, one of the candidates regularly aired a television chart depicting a rise in spending of tax dollars in an attempt to portray himself favorably in relation to the incumbent governor. The incumbent objected strenuously, arguing distortion of the data.

What an opportunity for civic service for the students in the state's 66 academic high schools. What a good lesson in math to take the same raw data and build an appropriate graph. What a good lesson in history to understand the manipulation of data for political purposes.

What a good lesson in civics for each student to determine which candidate best understood that our democracy can establish justice only through a respect for truth.

Students: "Ensure the Domestic Tranquillity"

- Help fellow teenagers avoid unwed pregnancies.
- Get safe adult help for children whose home environments are hostile, violent, incestuous.
- Help fellow students avoid unwanted sex.
- Help fellow students throw off depression, calm disturbing fears, and avoid suicide as a solution.
- Provide a confidential forum for peer discussion and wholesome service activities leading to positive self-images.
- Reach out to those with physical and mental problems to ensure their happiness.
- Insist that children be included in neighborhood crime watch plans.
- Help fellow teenagers avoid drinking and driving.

A reader might well ask what any of this has to do with government per se. And why I have chosen to use phrases out of context from the Preamble to the U.S. Constitution.

I do so because an enormous percentage of social studies teachers nationwide asks students to read—perhaps even to commit to memory—these phrases, yet they seldom connect the meanings of these phrases to the democratic well-being of our republic. Hence, what I have attempted to do is suggest some activities that an alert teacher might use to help make the study of government more meaningful.

One half of all births in the United States in 1990 were to teenagers; half of those to unwed teens. Furthermore, some 50% of all school children live in one-parent families.

We're now placing the fourth generation of welfare-dependent children in our public schools.

This means that 45 years ago a great many women with an inadequate economic base gave birth to at least one child. That child grew up dependent on welfare checks. Statistics show that before this child's 20th birthday, a second-generation child was born, growing up with more than a 50% chance of staying within the welfare system. Next, the third-generation, welfare-dependent child was born to a teenager. Today, that child, still welfare dependent and while a teenager, has given birth to an infant soon to enter the U.S. public school system. That fourth-generation little one lives in a domestic situation that has been dependent for economic security on poverty-level public funds for more than 40 years. Poor health, low-level work and literacy skills, and inadequate schooling and mentoring from those who can support dreams of personal success and economic independence have produced a cycle of failure that sorely needs breaking.

Children can help such children; together they can face a more hopeful future. Together they can look for ways to support each other's learning abilities and styles so that home circumstances don't limit possibilities or stifle interests and skills.

Does your school publicly identify those children eligible to receive free or reduced-cost meals? Why? How does that help either the child who needs the financial help or the child who does not? What lesson in democracy does that teach? No student I have asked about this labeling of students eligible for free school meals has ever agreed that this is right or fair.

Many of the school children I meet are better small "d" democrats than those who run their schools. They would not so humiliate their peers, and I would argue that the children know why: It has to do with *justice* and *tranquillity.*

Homework assignments are enormously effective in supporting the cycle of school failure for children living at or below the poverty line. How's that? Homework assignments *support* the cycle of failure? I am not alone in making the claim that hundreds of thousands of homework assignments regularly given out by teachers from Grade 4 on are guaranteed to promote the welfare-dependent cycle.

All a teacher needs to do is give for homework an assignment that requires home skills and support materials missing from one or more homes, and the statements in the paragraph above are rendered true. Because this is what the majority of teachers regularly do, we have every reason to suggest that community service, to ensure domestic tranquillity, should include peer tutoring, homework hotlines, home tutoring services, cooperative learning assignments, experiential learning experiences, and a service-learning curriculum.

Contracts. They are becoming popular. Each student, his or her parents or guardians, and school authorities agree on a year or marking period's course of study and attendant behaviors. All contracts should include community service activities—even internships—and include the work site supervisor as a collaborator on the final evaluation of each student's contracted work. Learning how to honor a contract is a strong first step in understanding the contract between those elected to public office and the electorate.

H Is for Helping

CITIZENS: MADE NOT BORN

A lost opportunity is the greatest of losses. Whittier mourned it as what "might have been." We own no past, no future, we possess only now. If the reliable now is carelessly lost in speaking or in acting, it comes not back again. . . . Faith in divine Love supplies the ever-present help and now, and gives the power to "act in the living present."

The dear children's good deeds are gems in the settings of manhood and womanhood. The good they desire to do, they insist upon doing now. They speculate neither on the past, present, nor future, but, taking no thought for the morrow, act in God's time.

Good deeds are immortal, bringing joy instead of grief, pleasure instead of pain, and life instead of death.

—Mary Baker Eddy

In truth, this entire book is about helping and about forging class-room service activity connections. Following are just a few of the many examples I've found that appear to help agency directors and school officials move from classroom-only schooling to a service-learning curriculum.

Example

A junior high student, involved with the Early Adolescent Helper Program in New York City, explains,

> On Tuesdays and Thursdays, we go in pairs to the Jewish Home and Hospital for the Aged to meet some of the residents. It's a great feeling to be with people who are always glad to see you and can tell you interesting stories of their pasts.
>
> On the last Tuesday of every month, the Jewish Home has a birthday party for the residents. There's entertainment and cake for the residents. We help serve the food and talk to them. When it's over we help escort them back to their rooms.
>
> On Thursdays, we sing songs from the movie *The Sound of Music*. We will do the play with some of the residents. In the play, each of us shares a role with a resident. Together we act and sing as one. We relax and enjoy ourselves. It takes responsibility and it's fun.

Related Academics

For History or Social Studies. Compare stories told by the elderly with knowledge gained from reading assignments and class discussions.

For English and Language Arts. Write essays about the historical implications of what has been learned from the elderly; write poetry about the encounters; compose original one-act plays in which a senior citizen and a student play a part together.

For Music. Compose original lyrics, teach them to the elderly, and sing them together.

Example

A participant at a Teen Institute training camp in San Diego writes,

The Teen Institute helps people with personal and family relationships, school performance, self-esteem, and, most of all, the prevention of alcohol and substance abuse. Teen Institute promotes the positive attitudes and the healthy environment we all need to better our communities.

Related Academics

For Health Class. Learn what best promotes a substance-free (and substance-controlled) person, home, environment, or community; learn to research health issues in medical research materials.

For English. Learn to write promotion copy for mass media aimed at the teen audience; learn to write publishable letters to the editor to support your substance abuse projects; learn to write memorandums explaining to specific audiences what needs to be done to promote a healthy environment.

Example

A high school senior from Burlington, Vermont, testifying before Senator Ted Kennedy's Committee on Health and Human Services, explained that she had recruited 100 of her classmates to help her plan an alcohol- and drug-free graduation party. When the senator asked her why she was doing this type of community service, she responded, "Three friends of mine were seriously hurt on graduation night a couple of years ago in an alcohol-related accident. I made up my mind I'd do everything I could to help my classmates do better."

Related Academics

For Speech Class. Learn to squeeze 10 minutes into 2 minutes; learn to express ideas in understandable images; learn to project voice and meaning for emphasis and control.

For Social Studies. Learn how to read the *Congressional Journal*; do research on past committee issues and decisions; develop an understanding of the purpose of congressional committee structure.

Example

Concern for the environment led scores of students from San Francisco area schools to clean up Ocean and Baker beaches in September 1990, removing debris weighing some 3,500 pounds.

Related Academics

For Science Courses. Using data cards, catalogue debris—as did the San Francisco students—for study in science courses, including a study of salinity and pollution rates.

For English. Learn to write position papers on a single issue like this one for presentation to a single audience.

For Social Studies. Learn what methods best promote a clean environment along beaches. Study city, county, state, and federal regulations regarding beach environments. Learn how to influence legislation regarding beach pollution.

Example

Older students in some California high schools volunteer to be lab assistants in math resource labs, helping to plan, prepare, and teach arithmetic lessons to elementary school students who have asked for such help. Considerable effort is made to match the language and cultural backgrounds of the tutors and their pupils.

Example

I was having a discussion with a group of junior and senior high school students about ways they could improve the health of their community through providing services for elderly adults. One student seemed skeptical about the need for such services, stating, "All the old people I know are doing just fine on their own." I was stumped for a moment and filled the silence with an old-fashioned remark: "Goodness me."

More silence, then one of the boys spoke up: "I go to an older person's home every Thursday for 2 hours and do chores for her she couldn't do herself. She's pretty frail and has failing eyesight. I get wood in for her stove, move heavy bags so the trash people can pick them up, sometimes get things down for her from top shelves, things like that."

The skeptic asked how he'd found her, and he answered, "My mother is a visiting nurse. She could tell you about at least 20 more people who need your help."

The skeptic again: "Does the old lady pay you?"

"Oh, no. Well, not if you mean money. You see, we spend some time talking together. She's really interested in me and what I'm learning in school. And, of course, she always has some cookies and milk for me. I didn't sign up for spring baseball last year because I wanted to be with her at least once a week. She's not going to be around forever, and I need to learn more from her about how to be patient and things like that."

Related Academics

For Interdisciplinary Study. Teachers and parents need to support student discussions and reflective thinking on both the moral and the spiritual meanings of acts that promote personal and community health.

Students, in keeping their journals, should be encouraged to write truly private and personal comments, knowing they will not be subjected to grammar and spelling checks. But these journal notes might well form the basis for discussions with peers and adults, helping them to think about—and to compare their ideas with—what great leaders have done and thought in similar circumstances.

Example

A woman, whose house lay on the school bus route of a "tough student," did not have her rural mailbox shoveled free of snow one winter, hampering mail delivery. The "toughie" remarked how thoughtless this was of the old lady living there. "Dumb broad, doesn't even have the decency to clear the snow out of there for the mailman."

Then he learned that the woman had recently undergone surgery and had one arm removed. Onto the bus the very next day went an old snow shovel; at the boy's command (no, not a request!) the bus driver stopped. In moments the area was cleared. The shovel was stowed in the back of the bus. When he left school that year, he assigned a younger student to "keep that mailbox clear." Then he added, "Look in the box. She puts chocolate chip cookies in there after every storm."

Related Academics

For Civics Class. Learning the interrelationships between civic rights and civic responsibilities. The rights of citizenship vary from town to town and state to state; so do the responsibilities. Many of the issues facing local communities are ones that seriously affect the lives of the children; hence, involving students early in learning to balance what's allowed with what's required creates not only helpers but also problem solvers.

I Is for Interns

CITIZENS: MADE NOT BORN

A commitment to active citizenship and community service has always been an American characteristic. That commitment, which has fostered and preserved our democracy for over 200 years, now seems to be weakening among young people. It is up to everyone in a position of leadership—particularly educators—to help reverse this trend.

Part of the problem lies in the fact that one can go through a full and supposedly thorough formal education without ever hearing or reading about the major role the voluntary sector plays in American life. Alan Pifer, president emeritus of the Carnegie Corporation, reviewed more than 50 textbooks used in civics, history, social studies, and the like and found no reference to philanthropy or to voluntary organizations.

—Brian O'Connell

Intern

"Resident within" (from the French, according to *Webster's 2nd College Edition*). Synonyms include apprentice, novice, and learner.

35

It would be delightful if every appropriate service agency (where confidentiality and safety are not serious problems) would ask local high schools for student interns, agreeing to oversee compatible course work during a full-time internship of at least 6 weeks' duration.

A student seriously interested in botany, planning either to leave school and work in a florist shop or nursery or to go on to college and major in botany, might spend a marking period working in a local hospital's greenhouse as a volunteer, doing an independent study project for full course credit, and receiving a grade for the quality of the internship work from the hospital supervisor.

A student seriously interested in music, planning either to leave school and work in the music field or to go on to college and major in some aspect of music, might spend a marking period helping a local school music teacher or a community choral group or orchestra, receiving credit from school for a related independent study project and a grade for the quality of the internship work.

A student interested in a business career, planning either to leave school and begin full-time employment or to go on to major in business at college, might intern in the office of the local United Way.

A student doing poorly in course work might be given an opportunity to intern at a nonprofit agency alongside a highly motivated, high-scoring fellow student, receiving peer tutoring and counseling and being graded for an independent study project by a teacher, the peer tutor, and the work supervisor.

Suggested reading: Chapter 4 of *Seeds: Some Good Ways to Improve Our Schools* (Parsons, 1985) and Chapter 2 of *The Co-op Bridge* (Parsons, 1991).

If a school teacher has never had an internship experience, it's very difficult to imagine how this way of learning can enhance a student's course of study. School administrators might provide short-term internships for teachers in local service agencies, those agencies with which their pupils could intern. For example, a homeless shelter. The teacher intern might work in the budget office, streamline the food service operation, or develop writing and reading classes. This would not only give the teacher practice as an intern but also reveal ways students might take advantage of a community need to develop important academic skills.

J Is for Justice

CITIZENS: MADE NOT BORN

Beginning in elementary and high school, boys and girls should learn to take some responsibility for the well-being of any group they are in—a seemingly small step but without doubt the first step toward responsible community participation. And for that matter, the first step in leadership development. On the playing field and in group activities in and out of school, teamwork can be learned. Through volunteer and intern experiences outside of school they learn how the adult world works and have the experience of serving their society. Every organization serving the community should find ways of involving young people.

I take the same view of [the] claim that leaders are born, not made that Dr. Samuel Johnson took of cucumbers, which he said should be carefully sliced, well seasoned with pepper and vinegar, and then thrown out.

—John W. Gardner

Thomas Jefferson said,

> I know no safe depository of the ultimate powers of the society but the people themselves; and if we think them not enlightened enough to exercise their control with a wholesome discretion, the remedy is not to take it from them, but to inform their discretion. (from a letter to Charles Jarvis, September 28, 1820)

Treasured Rights

One of the treasured rights of all U.S. citizens, including its children, is the principle that one is innocent until proven guilty. Another treasured right is trial by jury, with the further requirement that the plaintiff must prove the defendant guilty, rather than the defendant prove himself innocent. It is the rare public school, even the rare secondary school—some of the pupils of which will be old enough to be judged as adults by the courts—that considers its students "enlightened enough to exercise . . . control with a wholesome discretion." But if one believes former President Jefferson, the remedy is not to deny our youngsters the opportunity to control themselves "but to inform their discretion" by education.

Discretion

Roget's Thesaurus provides the words *diplomacy, circumspection, thoughtfulness, tact, caution, prudence, foresight, sagacity, responsibility,* and *maturity* as equivalents for the word discretion.

We need to nurture these qualities through education. Let me cite as an example how this was done in a private boarding school, for upper elementary and junior high students needing some special academic help, located on the outskirts of a primitive forest area in the mountains of Southern California.

It was my second year as a teacher and my first in this school. One lad had distinguished himself as its most unruly and destructive student. At the first staff meeting, the director, a woman of enormous skill and insight into this age group, suggested that this youngster be asked to serve on a volunteer rescue squad.

As one, the staff tried to argue her out of the idea. She overruled us, stating, "You'll see, he'll rise to the responsibility; he's just acting this way because he's homesick and afraid and doesn't want anyone to know it." She was correct; he did "rise to the responsibility."

In fact, he showed such discretion—tact, sagacity, and responsibility—that the members of the rescue squad, at their next election, made him their chief.

Judged by Peers

A few years later, at a different school, another troubled youth—fully grown and old enough to serve in the armed forces—had done all that he could think of to get himself thrown out of school. But that school had a student court. The 12 peers first listened to the plaintiff's complaints about him, then, assuring the young man that he was still considered innocent, asked him to defend himself against the charges. He made no effort to gloss over his many unruly and impolite encounters with teachers, administrators, and even fellow pupils but went on to explain how badly he needed tutoring in some basic skills and how particularly frustrated he was by the gap between his ability at mechanical work on the one hand and literary work on the other.

Tutors were found. His reading and writing skills improved dramatically. In 6 months he was elected president of the student body. Asked why he supported his friend's candidacy, the former president explained, "You just wait and see, he'll really clean up, and by gosh, he'll be fair because he knows what it's like when people aren't fair." As student body president, his first act was to make peer tutoring available to every student.

Also, this newly elected president was able to convince the school authorities to let almost all discipline cases be heard by a student jury, with verdicts and punishments meted out by the students, not by the vice principal.

Jury After Jury After Jury

J is for Justice. And of all the areas of civic instruction, the one in which I believe our U.S. schools fall down the most is that of teaching justice by allowing students to learn how to be just. Of all the areas where learning by doing is key to understanding, it is most so in that of justice. Above all, there must be choice, discretion, and tact. Evidence must be weighed. Motives must be assessed. Special circumstances must be addressed.

You couldn't learn to get the basketball into the hoop 8, 9, or 10 times out of 10 tries by reading about basketball, discussing basketball, reviewing films about basketball, or listening to tapes made by the top basketball players of all time. No, you'd need to throw a basketball at a hoop over and over and over. The instances are not entirely comparable, but youngsters couldn't learn how to serve on a jury just by reading about juries, discussing juries, reviewing films of juries, or listening to tapes by legal experts on jury duty. No, they would need to be on jury after jury after jury.

Bill of Rights

Do you know about the Constitutional Rights Foundation and its *Bill of Rights in Action* newsletter? (601 South Kingsley Drive, Los Angeles, CA 90005). They have been performing a magnificent service, suggesting all sorts of service-learning opportunities to strengthen civic understanding—that is, to help make small "d" democrats.

The fall 1990 edition of the newsletter highlights the Eighth Amendment: "Excessive bail shall not be required, nor excessive fines imposed, nor cruel and unusual punishments inflicted." I know of a stupid and unusual punishment often inflicted on older high school students. A student age 16 or older drops out of school and then decides, probably through mentoring, that he should go back, only to be told by the school principal that before reentering he must do X hours of community service as punishment.

What a perverse message this sends to students about their place in a democracy, about what community service has to do with strengthening our republic, and about what schooling itself is for. Instead, what should happen is the provision of special support, as well as an opportunity to connect learning with service to enrich both.

K Is for Kindness

CITIZENS: MADE NOT BORN

May it please your honor, I will never pay a dollar of your unjust penalty [$100 and court costs]. . . . In your ordered verdict of guilty [for voting illegally] you have trampled under foot every vital principle of our government. My natural rights, my civil rights, my political rights, my judicial rights, are all alike ignored. Robbed of the fundamental privilege of citizenship, I am degraded from the status of a citizen to that of a subject; and not only myself individually but all of my sex are, by your honor's verdict, doomed to political subjection under this so-called republican form of government.

Your denial of my citizen's right to vote, is the denial of my right of consent as one of the governed, the denial of my right of representation as one of the taxed, the denial of my right to a trial by a jury of my life, liberty, property.

—Susan B. Anthony, c. 1872

Barry F. Sullivan was, in 1990, chairman and chief executive officer of First Chicago Corporation and also chairman of the board of trustees of the University of Chicago. Through the kindness of Hannah Grey, president of the university and a part-time Vermonter, I receive the university's official *Record*. The October 1990 issue includes the "Remarks" of Mr. Sullivan to degree recipients of the Graduate School of Business on June 8, 1990. He makes a compelling case for kindness.

We Have Met the Solution

Mr. Sullivan defines this decade's significant challenges and states, taking off from cartoon character Pogo, "that we have met the *solution*, and it is us." The challenges? ". . . the aging of our society— most notably, the dramatic increase in the proportion of [female] Americans over 75 years of age. Another is the need to integrate the growing number of energetic new immigrants into the mainstream of our society." He continues,

> When it comes to integrating minorities into every aspect of our society, laws have done what they can. The rest is up to us, as individuals. Not only do corporations have to "step forward"; we, as individuals, have to do so ourselves. I am referring to what I see as the obligation that each of us has to "reinvest," on an ongoing basis, in a society that offers us the stunning array of opportunities that our country does. What do I mean by "reinvest"? I mean that we need to be volunteers in our nation's schools, in our religious institutions, in our cultural organizations, and in our social welfare agencies that work with youth, the elderly, and the homeless.

Of course, Mr. Sullivan is talking about adults, not about children. But can't children do something about the challenge of an aging population, about the new wave of immigrants seeking the "promised land" or about discriminatory practices persistently inhibiting progress for Native Americans and African Americans?

We Had the Privilege

April Wege, a Tumwater (Washington) High School student, wrote in the *Service Line Newsletter,*

> We had the privilege of tutoring Abdu Adam, a Cambodian immigrant, to help prepare him for his naturalization test to become a U.S. citizen. It was truly a joy for us to work with him over two weeks, and to watch his awareness of U.S. government and the role of a U.S. citizen grow. Abdu worked very hard; the culmination of his efforts came when he passed his test on the first attempt.
>
> We ourselves experienced a development of character as high school students who used what we had learned to help change the life of another individual. This citizenship project, which we had undertaken as part of our civics class, was one of the highlights of our educational experiences.

I love the idea of every civics class sponsoring and tutoring at least one immigrant each term. I can just imagine the kindness the children would show to someone struggling to understand the principles of democratic government and its special form in the United States. And readily imagine how much more civics would be learned by the students because of the need to make things clear for another.

We Could Do Something for Them

When I asked some 30 elderly folk living in a variety of circumstances if they would like school students to provide some voluntary service for them, to a person they countered with, "Only if we could do something for them." This reminded me of what happened one winter night in a big eastern city.

It was bitter cold. Something went wrong with the electrical system in a residential section of the city, and more than 50,000 residents were without heat or electricity. Hundreds were elderly people living alone in large apartment houses—no water (no electricity to pump the water), no heat from any electric source, no lights on the city streets.

The Red Cross arrived with tents, generator-powered spotlights, a supply of blankets, and hundreds of sandwiches. As if by magic (no radio or TV announcements without power), hundreds of students arrived and went in coed pairs from apartment to apartment, bringing food, blankets, and comfort. A group of girls began caroling; soon some of the apartment residents came out and joined them. It was more than 48 hours before full power was restored.

Students were there every minute of every day unrequested and uncompensated financially. When asked why, they answered, "We love being here."

Among those the students helped was a former musician, now nearly blind, one of whose visitors was a budding pianist. A friendship was formed, and the student, who needed a piano to practice on, continued to visit for the next 2 years, learning from his elderly friend and giving him new reason to stay alive and alert.

A former schoolteacher, confined with a dog she thought was her only friend, became a grammarian-in-residence to a student group for whom English was a second language, after one who brought her a needed blanket used a verb in the plural with a singular subject.

Two-Way Kindness

Kindness isn't a one-way action; it demands a reciprocal relationship. Kindness is grace, compassion, support, and true philanthropy. A young black friend of mine turned a corner on a city street to find that two elderly white women had just had their purses snatched and their groceries scattered all over the sidewalk and into the street. He couldn't catch the thieves; they had gone off in a car. But he could help the two ladies, one of whom had had her glasses crushed and needed some guidance to negotiate the curbs and rough pavement.

My young friend was outraged. He gathered up as many of the groceries as he could, offered his arm to the lady with the broken eyeglasses, and took both women directly to their apartment in a low-cost housing project. He told them he didn't want them going to the grocery store without an escort, explained that he hung out regularly in a nearby youth drop-in center, and went on to say that they should ask for him so that he could go to the store with them. For many who knew my young friend, and the social and economic pressures on him, those women actually rescued him from similar uncivil, unlawful behavior.

They learned to love him; he learned to love them. He found reasons to come by and help them out with household chores. They taught him the joys of punctuality, consistency, and frugality. He gave them a strong reason to believe in desegregation.

Why Not Help?

I met with a group of high school students, half of whom had done some community service. The other half were there because I requested students who particularly did not want to do any voluntary service. Why not? Why, I asked, didn't they want to help out around town? They first talked about the fact that punishment in their school for breaking the rules was X hours of so-called community service, and they didn't want to do "punishment" work.

They had another reason. They didn't want to help people who should be helping themselves. This provided an opportunity for the other students to speak up and tell about their voluntary service activities, how much they enjoyed doing them, and how what they did was something the person couldn't do for himself, for example, the bed patient in restraints who could not feed himself or the frail elderly person unable to carry firewood into the house.

As we talked, suddenly those who had never shown practical kindness to a neighbor began asking how they could find and help those like their fellow students were helping.

L Is for Like What? and Liability

CITIZENS: MADE NOT BORN

Had I, during my residence in the United States, seen any single feature in their national character that could justify their never-ending boast of generosity and love of freedom, I might have respected them, however much my taste was offended by their peculiar manners and customs. But it is impossible for any person not to be upset by the contradictions between their principles and practice. They attack the governments of Europe, because as they say, they favor the powerful and oppress the weak. You may hear this said in Congress, roared out in taverns, discussed in every living room, poked fun at upon the stage, even discussed in the churches. Listen to it, and then look at them at home. You will see them with one hand lifting the cap of liberty, and with the other whipping their slaves. You will see them one hour lecturing their mob on the rights of man, and the next driving from their homes the Indians, whom they have bound themselves to protect by the most solemn treaties.

—Frances Trollope, c. 1832

That ungrammatical "like what?" comes from my many discussions with both school officials and managers of nonprofit organizations. As I begin to explore whether either would permit students to do some community service, particularly service integrated with academic course work, the question invariably arises: "Like what?"

Principals. If you knew how to lower the teacher-pupil ratio at no additional cost to the school district, wouldn't you do so? Use adult volunteers as classroom aides, as homework helpers, as mentors, as work supervisors, as intern managers, as phone pals, or as pen pals.

Students. Are you worried that your grades will go down, your rank in class will slip, and your standardized test scores won't make it into the 90th percentile; hence you will not be admitted to the college of your choice if you combine service and study? Not to worry; the most selective U.S. colleges and universities give preference in admissions to students who have done community service, particularly service integrated with the school curriculum.

Some Interesting Service-Learning Activities

Mary Ann Johnson is the director of the Illinois Governor's Office of Senior Involvement and, in 1990, held a series of meetings throughout the state, referred to as "The Circle of Helping," out of which has come an excellent report, titled *Intergenerational Service-Learning: Strategies for the Future* (Angelis, 1990). The following are just a few success stories culled from that report.

- A retired secretary assisted a high school business class. When she suffered a stroke, the students visited her and helped her through rehabilitation.
- Members of a fraternity helped some senior citizens relocate to a new building. The following semester, those senior citizens helped guide freshman students through the chaos of their first weeks at college.

- An older couple visited a preschool to read and tell stories to the children. Three years later, when one member lost his sight, the students took turns reading to him, proudly demonstrating their new skills.

- Retirees visited a youth center to tutor delinquent boys, who, in turn, shoveled snow for the retirees.

- Some preschool children visit a senior day care center every Tuesday at 10 a.m., engaging in activities with the seniors that are planned by the staffs of both institutions. The active seniors visit the preschoolers once a month for special theme programs; the preschoolers make tray decorations for those seniors served by Meals on Wheels.

- At one elementary school, all school programs are open to a nearby nursing home, which regularly receives a school activities newsletter written and compiled by the pupils, telling the senior residents of upcoming events. Students have pen pals in the nursing home and do joint gardening activities. In addition, the school band, orchestra, and chorus regularly hold performances at the nursing home.

- A nice twist: Residents at a nursing home compile a book for the students: *To the Youth of the 1990s From the Youth of the 1900s.*

- Students at one school fill out an "interest card." The RSVP (Retired Senior Volunteer Program) pairs each student with a senior citizen with similar interest, starting off the relationship at a potluck supper.

- A retired teachers association and a local branch of the American Association of University Women hold regular 90-minute homework help sessions for any student needing assistance.

- Homebound seniors call the RSVP and place their grocery orders. Volunteers from the home economics classes and an RSVP volunteer do the shopping, then the students deliver the groceries and stay to help put them away and have a short visit.

- Students read stories on a radio broadcast for the blind.

- Bilingual students offer telephone pal service to adults in the non-English-speaking community on a daily basis.

- From 3 to 6 p.m. every weekday, latchkey children may call and talk with a homebound senior who mediates sibling rivalries, listens to the day's events, and answers homework questions. The seniors have all the information needed to get emergency service to a latchkey child.
- A local library holds its Saturday morning children's story hour in a nursing home, reading to both audiences.
- A school hosts a volunteer day, asking students to tell how they could use an adult volunteer. Each student or group of students sets up a table in the cafeteria, and older community residents are invited to visit each table and, if interested, sign on as a volunteer. For example, maybe the school chess club is looking for more players, or the school chorus needs a couple of strong bass voices, or the art students want a show juried.

How?

I'm delighted to report that since the first edition of this book was published in 1991, the question is no longer "Like what?" Instead, the query from school officials today is "How?" We've advanced nationwide from wondering just what voluntary community service is to the very progressive step of wondering just how to ensure that the service is meaningful and complementary to age-appropriate academic study.

Schoolteachers. Avoid as you would carriers of the Black Plague those "experts" in service learning who lecture about how you should not lecture and fill large pads of paper with brainstorming lists instead of providing you with problem-solving coaching in the whys and wherefores of how service can be integrated with the curriculum.

Call on sincere experiential teachers to lead you in workshops and service-learning courses. Use peer coaching to learn from each other how you've been able to enhance course work with service work. Experiment. Use professional time to learn from agency supervisors how they make *best* use of student volunteers. There is a national toll-free number (1-800-808-7378) operated by the National Service-Learning Clearinghouse, which maintains a database of reference information.

The Liability Question

Almost all public school districts as well as private schools carry liability insurance that covers students and staff while on school outings. Students whose voluntary service is not school related may not, in fact, be covered by the school's insurance policies. But those engaged in service that is school related are generally covered, and liability should not be a concern.

It is also true that a great many organizations that use student and adult volunteers carry liability insurance; hence pupils who are carrying out a service-learning project in a hospital, a nursing home, a town recreation center, and the like may be covered by both the school insurance and the organization's insurance.

For example, youngsters who are taken to service-learning jobs in the backseat of the driver education automobile are covered, as of course are all those who travel by school bus from school to site to home. For some activities, as for certain field trips, it might be necessary to have parents and guardians sign a waiver exempting the school, the organization, or both from liability. But that is rare and generally involves older students doing internships in exotic locations.

M Is for Money

CITIZENS: MADE NOT BORN

True, the heart grows rich in giving;
All its wealth is living grain;
Seeds which mildew in the garner,
Scattered, fill with gold the plain.
Is thy burden hard and heavy?
Do thy steps drag wearily?
Help to bear thy brother's burden,
God will bear both it and thee.
Is the heart a well left empty?
None but God its void can fill;
Nothing but a ceaseless fountain
Can its ceaseless longings still.
Is the heart a living power?
Self-entwined its strength sinks low;
It can only live in loving,
And, by serving, love will grow.

—Elizabeth Charles

---

1. How much should a school district of, say, 10,000 students reasonably expect to budget for service learning?

2. How much should a high school of 500 students expect to allocate in its budget to support its voluntary student service programs?

3. Would an elementary school serving 500 pupils need more or less money to support service learning than the same size secondary school?

4. Should a school district, contemplating its first student community service program, expect that although the initial start-up costs will be high, subsequent costs will be negligible?

5. Is it possible that the introduction of service learning in a school system could lower, not raise, overall per-pupil costs?

Question 5

Let me answer the fifth question first—Yes. Good service learning, as I trust this book is demonstrating, is a two-way street. Students studying a foreign language, who become pen pals of those for whom the students' second language is their first, have added that many more teachers to the system at no additional cost to the school district. There will need to be fewer texts, fewer audiocassettes, fewer trips abroad, fewer field trips, and the teacher-pupil ratio will be lowered.

Peer teaching reduces the need for substitute teachers, aides, paraprofessionals, part-time instructors, and paid tutors.

Learning horticulture while caring for flora in public parks, nursing home gardens, school landscaped areas, and community centers—particularly if undertaken with the assistance of the local garden club—would reduce the cost of school grounds maintenance—and would considerably reduce the cost of in-school laboratory space and equipment.

Using students to help staff in-school day care centers, after-school latchkey programs, and breakfast and snack programs and to monitor the school hotline would create a considerable saving overall.

Questions 1, 2, and 3

And now let me return to the earlier questions, first making some generalizations. Just as the coach of a specific sport receives both extra pay for coaching and reduced classroom assignments, a community service coordinator should be given time and "extra" pay.

This coordinator may need a telephone line, a one-time cost. This coordinator may need a part-time clerk or secretary, a recurring cost. This coordinator may need a budget to pay out-of-pocket expenses for certain community service projects, also a recurring cost.

There may be a need for special insurance coverage. Transportation costs, particularly in rural areas, may be an additional recurring expense.

But let's answer Questions 1, 2, and 3 with the same figure: $10 per pupil.

Question 4

This question doesn't have a ready answer. Too much depends on decisions made at either the school or the school district level. Such a decision might be to ask one teacher to involve one class and to have just one culminating community service event the first year. Or the position of community service coordinator could be made a separate post and filled with a highly paid employee or staffed with a secretary supported by a team of consultants.

Most important of all, though, is the fact that the way school funds are budgeted—as soon as service learning is part and parcel of the entire school program—will change dramatically. There needn't be more money, but clearly, a different distribution of the funds on hand will be required.

Because students will be working under agency supervision part of the time, fewer full-time-equivalent teachers may be necessary, saving funds needed for such things as special equipment and rotating bus service between school and work sites.

It may be hard for many school officials to believe, but those who have begun to add service learning to the school syllabus discover that money isn't nearly the factor they had imagined; instead, commitment to the concept is what's most needed—and in many instances, most lacking.

N Is for Natural Science

CITIZENS: MADE NOT BORN

Public service . . . is advocated as a way to connect educational values with community action in a reciprocal relationship. Important links can be forged between students and society much to the advantage of both. Students are exposed to real-life situations and conditions of human need, and the community gains dedicated, well-educated volunteers.

In the coming years, I expect animated debate over the educational needs essential to our democracy.

—Adele Simmons

- Produce a weekly engagement calendar (proceeds going to the nonprofit agency or agencies of your choice), which features on its facing pages one natural science guesstimate made by a local senior citizen, for example, the first night when the temperature will drop below freezing, the first sighting of a monarch butterfly, the first sighting of migrating whales, and so on. Computer skills,

English, history, natural science, design, art, and photography could all be involved in producing the calendar.

- Provide care for all aquariums located in nonprofit settings, such as nursing homes, hospitals, senior centers, day care facilities, public libraries, and schools. Combine this care with science study at all school levels. Use the aquariums for research projects in college-preparatory biology and zoology as well as in general science classes. Perhaps do some statistical analysis, using computer skills; or write some literary prose and poetry, strengthening English composition skills. Use a resident of the facility as a research assistant. Bind the report and add it to the facility's library.

- Take pets from local humane societies for short-term visits to day care and senior centers, giving training to the pets, and providing cheer to the visitors. Combine this activity with science and English course work.

- Teach your community how to recycle. Is the local diner separating cardboard from general trash? What happens to the opened cans from the local chain restaurant? In all local condominium buildings and apartment complexes with built-in incinerators, are the residents separating newspapers, glass, computer paper, cardboard, cans? The project might combine general science with math, English, history, and computer skills.

- Work on legislation to protect the endangered species in your local area; learn about research being done to protect endangered species throughout the world. General science, math, English, and history could all be involved.

- Do something about local air quality. Monitor pollution levels from traffic, from industry, from private homes, from refuse centers. Do something about tobacco-related air quality. Do something about effluent-related air quality. Review legislation, research scientific knowledge, issue periodic reports, and help change long-standing habits. Integrate your scientific study with lessons in English, math, social sciences, and politics.

- Provide a natural science hotline to deal with the control of natural disasters.

- Provide a natural science homework hotline.
- Provide the local media with natural science lore on a regular basis.
- Ask elders in the community to share a natural science history of the area. Provide the results of interviews in video and book form for community use.
- Teach a lesson in natural science on tray liners made in art class.
- Plant trees and flowers on public land in the community.
- Offer to provide plant and pet care for senior citizens.
- Develop and maintain a school zoo.
- Develop and maintain a town nature trail.

O Is for Obligation

CITIZENS: MADE NOT BORN

The public purpose of institutionalizing public schooling was to shape the young to become an enlightened electorate—so that democracy could be maintained, and so that effective and responsible leaders could emerge irrespective of social class or racial, ethnic, and gender origins. If, indeed, we look realistically at the total job of the school, we must begin and end with its primary reason for being—the public purpose. It is our moral responsibility to accomplish, above all, this primary goal, and no understanding of limits can exclude it from our definition of what the total job of the school is and must be.

—Faustine C. Jones-Wilson

My thesaurus lists *obligation* as the first synonym for *mandatory*. And the following are listed as equivalents to the word obligation: *imperative, compulsory, mandatory, requisite, binding, required, enforced,* and *coercive*.

When I am asked if I believe student community service should be mandated or obligatory, I respond, "I think it's hard to learn how to volunteer in a mandatory program."

Yet school statistics offer much to support the idea of obligatory service. A survey taken in 1987, covering 1,000 schools, found that about 700 schools had some student community service activities ongoing. In 140 of the schools, service was mandatory and 100% of the student body was involved; in the remaining 560 schools, only a small percentage (never as much as 50% and often less than 10%) participated in cocurricular service clubs.

That's what makes me so fond of service learning. If the service and the course work are designed so that they support each other, then everyone in the course engages in service while engaging in learning. Yet in those schools that mandate service, generally it's not learning that is the goal, but hours. To graduate, so the regulation generally stipulates, a student must have "done" X hours of service.

But the debate over whether student community service should be voluntary or obligatory is the stuff of which democracy is made. I believe there's something wonderful about a democracy's struggles with this kind of issue, seeking ways to share a community's responsibilities. I think it's good for us all to be thus engaged: debating, exploring, airing, and reassessing such matters.

We all might at least go as far as Thomas Jefferson: "A debt of service is due from every man to his country proportioned to the bounties which nature and fortune have measured to him."

P Is for Physical Education

- A group of special-needs children and young adults is brought to a large secondary school every afternoon to join the physical education classes. The program is so popular that regular school students must sign up a week in advance to be among the host program participants.
- Residents living in a shelter for battered and abused women are brought during the day in small groups to middle and high schools to participate with students in classes in gymnastics, swimming, tumbling, folk dancing, and noncontact sports.

- Junior and senior high school students, for physical education credit, organize games and physical education lessons for children at a local elementary school.
- Senior citizens are invited to participate in special physical education classes such as aquatic exercise, figure skating, shuffleboard, archery, Ping-Pong, croquet, horseshoe pitching, and other noncontact sports.
- A middle school's cross-country ski trail is maintained by the physical education classes and used evenings, weekends, and vacations by the community.
- Schools cooperate with town sports leagues to share coaches.
- Community members who love to dance are invited to join physical education dance classes.
- Schools with swimming pools permit students to satisfy physical education requirements by offering swimming and diving lessons to preschoolers, handicapped youngsters, and senior citizens.
- In place of playing a team sport, older students coach younger children in the team sports at which the older students excel.

ℚ Is for Quid pro Quo

CITIZENS: MADE NOT BORN

Service is not just giving out, it is also gaining insights. There will be joy and satisfaction, and pain and frustration, too. In any event, if students are to be educationally affected by service, they should be asked to comment on their experience and explore with a mentor and fellow students how the experience is related to what they have been studying in school. . . . The goal is to help students consider the connection between what they learn and how they live.

—Ernest L. Boyer

Something for Something

Year after year, in polls taken to determine what parents consider to be the main failing of U.S. public schools, the problem of *discipline* is high on the list, if not first.

Polls show that the business community doesn't believe schools have taught entry-level workers basic skills or workplace discipline.

61

And, of course, polls of school teachers and administrators show that they believe that parents and taxpayers are not providing schools with adequate support.

Service learning is "something for something" to meet the demands of parents, business executives, and educators.

The antidote for poor behavior on the part of students is engagement in an activity of compelling interest: for instance, becoming a dance partner for a blind child or adult, which instills a deep desire for self-discipline. The antidote for poor workplace behavior and absent basic skills is the provision of opportunities to learn how to behave there and of basic-skills lessons through hands-on activity. The antidote for too few resources is to share teaching and applied-skill lessons with the wider community, lowering the teacher-pupil ratio and, in effect, securing up-to-date equipment through the work-study sites themselves.

But what about the quid pro quo for politicians? Today's buzz-word for those labeling themselves conservatives is *choice*. Give students and parents the means to choose the school that best fits their expectations, so say these politicians, and all schools will improve in an effort to retain a portion of the school market, and the range of choices will widen. Service learning is the personification of choice. The youngster who is studying mathematics and wants to gain experience with its use in budgeting and bookkeeping has a world of choice as to where to learn, from hundreds of nonprofit and commercial agencies.

The decision of where to do service can turn on location, personnel, skill development, pertinence to specific curriculum offerings, and so on. In other words, learning to serve and serving to learn display the entire philosophy of choice.

And what about the quid pro quo for students? Giving is getting; there's just no doubt about that. There may be rough patches at the beginning of some partnerships between students and those in need, but real gratitude begins the moment the school youngster finds a way to be truly helpful. And it's a lot more than warm chocolate chip cookies in exchange for clearing the snow from the base of a rural mailbox or grammar lessons for someone who brought a blanket on a cold night.

Something for a Head Start

A group of older teenagers—some 30 of them—had opted to take a special two-course-credit high school program that would put them in service locations for several hours each week. They would satisfy academic course credits by giving oral and written reports about their experiences.

They could choose where they would serve; today, it was the director of a local Head Start center who was addressing them. I was seated where I could watch the faces of the older teenage boys, and when the dark-colored, gray-haired, extremely thin administrator began her talk, student reactions ranged from boredom to rudeness.

But that soon changed. After the briefest of descriptions of why infants and toddlers needed a head start, she asked—ever so quietly yet ever so firmly—"Are there any young men here who could be a wholesome mentor for a fatherless little boy?"

She was relentless. She asked if there were any young men in the room who could help Head Start boys learn to appreciate their mothers, grandmothers, and aunts. She asked if any of the young men in the room had skill enough to read aloud to a Head Start boy from a classic in children's literature.

The young men squirmed. All of them. She continued describing how badly—particularly for the black boys—good role models were needed in the Head Start center, and she kept asking if there were no young black men willing to devote time to the children—time free of bad language, tobacco, alcohol, cynicism, and ignorance.

The atmosphere in the room changed drastically. All buffoonery ceased. The older black teenagers began raising their hands. Yes, they agreed, if they signed on they wouldn't be absent without serious cause, wouldn't get the hopes up for a little fellow and then dash them with indifference, wouldn't indulge in bad habits while with their Head Start youngster, and would be willing to take lessons in reading aloud.

Then she introduced the quid pro quo: "You will be doing something you're proud of." She continued, "You will be doing something you deserve to be proud of."

Something for Cultural Appreciation

A high school student became concerned about the way many in his community treated the tiny Native American population and, as a service-learning project, brought Indian lecturers and drummers to town. He helped the few Native Americans honor their own culture while helping the many local people honor the descendants of the "first Americans." It wasn't easy to go against a local stream of indifference— even hostility—but he persisted, and some gains were made.

To his delight, he won a prestigious Yoshiama Award from the Hitachi Foundation for his service-learning work and was also awarded a generous scholarship to the college of his choice based on his service record. Truly, something for something.

R Is for Recreation

CITIZENS: MADE NOT BORN

Did you too, O friend, suppose democracy was only for elections, for politics, and for a party name? I say democracy is only of use there that it may pass on and come to its flower and fruits in manners, in the highest forms of interaction between men, and their beliefs—in religion, literature, colleges and schools—democracy in all public and private life.

—Walt Whitman

School superintendents could save their communities a considerable amount of money by housing the parks and recreation offices in any one of the school buildings not already at capacity.

School officials could involve members of the community in physical education offerings, for instance, folk dancing, aquatic exercises, limbering-up movements done to music, or mild calisthenics.

Older students—perhaps those interested in careers in recreation—could serve as town recreation volunteers, integrating science classes with laboratory work in town gardens, park areas, and woods and in the design and building of nature trails. They might combine English composition assignments with the publication of a town recreation newsletter or art assignments with the design and production of outdoor sculptures, posters, art shows, and so on.

- Maintain a community recreation hotline. Groups of students, probably in association with a committee of adults, would take turns maintaining a community calendar of recreation opportunities for all age groups, either answering the calls themselves or preparing the taped messages. For a language arts assignment, produce a monthly recreation newsletter, collating all community recreation offerings to which the public is welcome. If there is a need for a translation of the newsletter into one or more languages other than English, integrate this work with foreign language study.

- Hold field days—sponsored by a school or a community—involving games at several skill levels. Mix on the same teams old and young, physically challenged and physically able, male and female, experienced and inexperienced.

- Plan the use of school athletic facilities as community recreation facilities, such as family ice skating on a flooded rink, folk dance lessons in the cafetorium for residents of homeless shelters, bird walks led by high school botany students through a town park, basketball clinics for women in their 30s, or coeducational volleyball tournaments organized by junior high students.

- Work closely with one or more community agencies to develop walking, cycling, skiing, jogging, running, and natural science trails. Let the student volunteers count this activity as physical education class.

- Is there an adult recreation committee appointed by some town official? Have one third of the members be school-age youngsters or have a second committee made up entirely of students, which reports to the adult committee.

- For all children who have had to be out of school for more than 5 days due to some illness, provide student volunteers to help with recreation and physical therapy.

- Have middle school students (10- to 14-year-olds) run latchkey recreation programs for 5- to 9-year-olds. High school students (15- to 20-year-olds) might run after-school recreation programs for middle school students who have no one at home to be with.

- With the aid of adults who belong to garden and local history clubs, have student interns produce printed guides for tours in recreation areas, offering these to tourists as well as to interested local residents. Such areas could include the public gardens, a town's forest area, a landscaped cemetery, or a river, lake, or major waterfront. The interns might be responsible for deciding the routes, mapping and describing them, designing and producing the maps and pamphlets, and keeping the distribution boxes stocked.

- Many older people want to do some daily walking but need to be out of inclement weather and in a safe environment. For physical education credit, have teams of students on hand to assist interested senior citizens in using hallways and available athletic areas of the school for walking exercise. Within each school, there are talented members of the faculty who have the background and knowledge to help strengthen recreation for all members of the community. In addition, student populations present a constantly renewable manpower base. What this should mean for every community is a recreation program available all day every day, designed to meet the needs of all segments of the population. Theater programs, crafts fairs, games of Capture the Flag, team sports played in skill-appropriate leagues, hiking trails, special summertime activities, Special Olympics for seniors and the handicapped—the list is as long as the recreation opportunities. What's needed today is for town officials to expect that talented school officials will guide recreation programs, using student volunteers who are developing academic skills because of their participation.

S Is for SerVermont

CITIZENS: MADE NOT BORN

First, there is the task of creating a school committed to enabling all—every last kid—to deal with powerful questions facing them in their society, to allow every kid to uncover . . . the fundamental, intellectual, and social issues of his or her time.

Second, there is the task of creating a school community that focuses on the developing and abiding interest in and commitment by our children to their community. We measure the success by the number who find ways to strengthen their family and their community.

Third, there is the task of creating a school that counts its success in its ability to create powerful participants in society, active citizens, not merely individual stars.

—Deborah Meier

A Bit of Background

In 1985, the Edwin Gould Foundation for Children gave me a yearlong study grant to see if I could determine why it was the United

States had no voluntary national service program. We had then, and have today, a volunteer armed services program, but we did not have then a program for domestic service with benefits akin to those offered for military service. During my year of exploration, I discovered that—with very few exceptions—no study of civics incorporated the doing of civic service in any of our public or private schools.

Children and young people could spend a dozen years in our schools and never do any community service or, if any was done, never have the connection made between the meaning of participatory democracy and the meeting of local community needs. It was no wonder there was so little enthusiasm for national service by those aged 18-plus.

Vermont's Beginnings

As soon as possible, I began talking with the governor of Vermont and the Commissioner of Education about helping the state's schools integrate some community service with academic course work. I didn't want to run a program or call for a mandate or push something through the legislature. Instead, I wanted teachers and administrators to decide among themselves how meeting local community needs could—uniquely—complement all academic studies, but particularly civics and government and social studies classes. SerVermont is an initiative, not a structured program. It is privately run and privately funded. As Governor Madeleine M. Kunin introduced it in her 1986 State of the State address,

> In this coming year, we will launch a volunteer program for high school students, stressing public service in the community, called "SerVermont."
>
> Students will be taught the value of personal volunteer service and our communities should benefit from their efforts.

SerVermont continues to be a volunteer program. It is no longer confined to the high school years but includes all of Vermont's kindergarten through Grade 12 students. Communities have benefited and are continuing to benefit from the voluntary service done by Vermont's youngsters.

SerVermont is a "carrot," not a stick. If anything distinguishes SerVermont from other school-related community service efforts, it is the strong emphasis on linking the service with the curriculum. SerVermont doesn't count hours or compute how much money has been "saved" at minimum wage by students doing X hours of service.

SerVermont doesn't advocate X hours of voluntary service as a graduation requirement, X hours as punishment, or X hours for those with high grade point averages. SerVermont believes schools should be thinking continually of ways they can help improve local communities and how students can practice learning how to be active community members. SerVermont does care whether the voluntary student service is direct, person to person; whether it is integrated with the curriculum; whether what is being done by the students is something the community believes needs doing.

SerVermont agrees with John Dewey: "Democracy has to be born anew every generation, and education is the midwife."

Professor Richard Remy uses learning how to ride a bicycle to explain how significant learning is acquired through doing:

> To develop such competence, a person must have the experience of actually riding a bicycle under a variety of conditions.
>
> One may prepare for the experience and contribute to one's proficiency by studying the physics involved in bicycle riding, by learning safety rules, or by studying the design of bicycles. Parents can structure the learning experience to increase the probability of success by providing advance instructions, training wheels, the proper size and type of bicycle, a safe area to ride, feedback on progress, and remedial instruction.
>
> But without continued practice, there is little likelihood that one will ever become a competent bicycle rider. (La Raus & Remy, 1978)

SerVermont adds this: Without civic service coupled with civics instruction, there is little likelihood that one will ever become a competent citizen.

T Is for Time and Transportation

CITIZENS: MADE NOT BORN

SerVermont Is a Dream

A Dream—that every student in Vermont's public schools will do some important community service.

A Dream—that every community will be enriched by the voluntary service done by its student-citizens.

A Dream—that each nonprofit organization in Vermont will train and use students to enhance the quality of service each one provides its clients.

A Dream—that each government agency in Vermont will make a place for student volunteers, thereby helping to bring civics and citizenship lessons alive.

A Dream—that parents and guardians will encourage and support student volunteers making it possible for them to learn by doing, that is, to learn how to be small "d" democrats.

A Dream—that school authorities will encourage and support students in community service as an essential part of free public schooling.

—Cynthia Parsons

"Toime"

I promised Vermont's governor and its education commissioner that I would not only start SerVermont's activities at the secondary school level but that I would begin in what Vermonters call the "Northeast Kingdom," that portion of the state with the lowest population and the weakest economy. I also promised them I would visit Vermont's 66 academic high schools. The first school I visited (Canaan Memorial High, for Grades 7 to 12) was in the farthest northeast corner, Canada to the north, New Hampshire to the east. After driving for 4 hours north through a major snowstorm, I waited some 2 hours on a wooden school chair for the principal to finish repairing the school boiler. "We don't have much time for this sort of thing," was his quick response when he returned to his office, still wiping the oil off his hands. After more talking from me he said, "I'll put your notice in one of my teacher's boxes; he likes to try new things."

That, which I thought a dead end, proved to be something very different. But as to exactly how, I beg your patience.

At school after school, the principal or the guidance counselor (when the principal didn't want to bother with me) explained that the students already had too much to do, what with classes, sports, homework, and either farm chores or 20-hour-a-week jobs.

At the suggestion that the volunteer work might double as homework or class work, I was more often than not shown the door.

At about the fifth or sixth school, the principal remarked as soon as I came in, "Sorry, Miss Parsons, but I've only got 10 minutes. We're having a fire drill." It took only the second such fire drill for me to realize that these school administrators were sure there was no time for service activities, but because the governor and commissioner had written to say how much they were in favor of SerVermont, they had resorted to a surefire (pun intended) way out of having to spend much time with me.

I returned to the governor after visiting some 20 schools, all in the northern half of the state. I informed her, "I'm sorry to report, Madeleine (yes, called her by her first name, as do both supporters and detractors throughout the state), that the Vermont secondary schools are out of 'toime.' " (Native Vermonters have a Vermont accent, not Down East Maine or Kennedy "Bahston," but their own blend: Time is "toy-em," and swallow the "em.")

Governor Kunin frowned: "Cynthia, the state has run out of what?" I answered, "Toime. There's no toime. Even if I offer $200 minigrants to defray expenses for service work, the students haven't got the toime to do any."

For a great many school officials, the mention of "community service" does not conjure up visions of students interacting with the community in a way that naturally supports the school curriculum; instead, their first reaction is negative, because they see this type of activity as taking away from class and study time, already a precious commodity.

Transportation

Actually, "no transportation" was nearly as often the excuse—such as, "Miss Parsons, even if I could squeeze more time into the schedule, and I cannot, how would I transport these kids? You got money for that?"

Of course, the few Vermont schools located in the center of a town didn't point to that barrier; but after all, Vermont is the most rural of the 50 states, and transportation is costly not only in dollars but also in time. It took visits to only three rural regional schools before I discovered one solution to the transportation excuse—driver education. There it was: a driver, plenty of insurance, a car with an empty backseat, and a student with the time to drive around the area.

I used it at the very next school, at which students in industrial arts previously had offered to fix appliances for the elderly and handicapped in the area if they could get the appliances to the school. Now there was a way—also a way for the repaired item to be returned to its owner by its fixer(s) and time for the showing of gratitude.

Also, many nonprofit organizations are only too willing to help with transportation, either bringing their population to school for special programs or arranging safe transportation for volunteer workers. In addition, the Red Cross, with RSVP drivers, is making its vehicles increasingly available for student community service programs.

And many a rural school is able to piggyback on bus runs to and from vocational centers, dropping students off at nonprofit work sites.

No Time or Transportation

One of the teachers at Canaan Memorial High was interested in doing something with a social studies class to improve instruction in art, history, and language arts. He did more with his $200 SerVermont minigrant than even I thought possible.

A local expert on period style in architecture agreed to teach the students what was important about several of Canaan's historic buildings, all within easy walking distance of the high school. A local quiltmaker agreed to teach the necessary design and sewing skills.

A video camera was borrowed from the school's audiovisual supplies, and the minigrant allowed purchase of tapes. After studying the buildings themselves and researching the architectural periods through the state library loan system, the students made a videotape. Copies were subsequently presented to the town library, the school library, the Vermont Historical Society, and the Vermont library system.

The quilt was a class project displaying the five buildings chosen by the students as the most important in Canaan. The centerpiece was the town's library and the quilt hangs there, a gift from the Canaan Memorial High students.

Like the planting of liberty elm trees by the interdisciplinary science-history class at Wilmington High School—which meant taking the time to plant, learn about where to plant, and research why a new strain of elm is necessary—the Canaan video really didn't take "extra" time but was extremely important learning time. By fusing the service with the learning, both were enhanced.

U Is for the United States of America

CITIZENS: MADE NOT BORN

[The true community is] a community of tribulation, and only because of that is it a community of spirit; it is a community of toil, and because of that it is a community of salvation. . . . They are communities only if they prepare the way to the promised land through the thickets of this pathless hour. . . . A community of faith truly exists when it is a community of work.

The real essence of community is to be found in the fact, manifest or otherwise, that it has a center. The real beginning of a community is when its members have a common relation to the center overriding all other relations.

—Martin Buber

A Remarkable Democracy

As this book has been pointing out, the United States of America is a remarkable democracy. No other nation on earth has ever made education available to every citizen at any age and of whatever

75

learning ability. But this is truly the case in the United States. If you are in prison, schooling is available. If you dropped out of school at whatever age, you can return at whatever age. You can go to school by watching TV, listening to the radio, through the mail, by attending night classes, workshops, seminars, or sitting in formal classrooms. You can go to school for an hour, a day, a week, a month, a semester, or a lifetime.

It took awhile, but just about all citizens over the age of 18—even women and blacks—may vote. We've not made voter registration as readily available as we should, and incredible to admit, very, very few of our high schools celebrate the 18th-birthday turning point for our youths by registering them to vote and congratulating them for reaching this critical milestone. But all citizens may vote, no matter what the losers in local, state, and federal elections may think about their qualifications. (I speak as one who lost two elections to represent Chester-Andover, Vermont, in the state legislature.)

And there would be little reason for this book if U.S. public schools had taken as seriously their mandate to "make" children into small "d" democrats as they have their mandate to "make" literate young adults who can lead productive lives. The purpose of this book is not to rehearse the reasons for how well—or how poorly—the public schools of the United States make literate adults, but there is substantial evidence that both what is taught and the manner in which it has been taught have put at risk as many as one out of every two children by the age of 16.

Fortunately, focusing the schools on better teaching of citizenship will not compete with the teaching of literacy, thus putting even more youngsters at risk, but service learning enhances and improves the teaching of basic literacy and scientific skills.

Learning by Doing

In fact, suggestions pouring forth from the citadels of higher education and successful business communities across the United States are calling for exactly the kinds of service-learning activities described in this book. Learning by doing is not a new teaching practice, but it has been progressively abandoned in classroom after classroom, partly because it has not been part of the syllabus at those colleges and universities certifying the nation's teachers. Even in vocational education training, in which work experience and study skills are more likely to be integrated, very little is done to provide future vocational school teachers with experience in fusing what's taught in course work with what's being learned on the job. In fact, for more than a quarter of a century, the federal government's vocational education funds have gone 98% for study unrelated to work and only 2% for cooperative education.

The result for the business community—including private non-profit and government employers—has been a need for immediate on-the-job training for almost all employees hired direct from K through 12 schools.

A good many education scholars believe that the nation's public schools need restructuring from the roots up and that they require a new form of government. Something clearly needs "fixing" when only one of two children who enter the public school system manages to become functionally literate; only one of four 18- to 25-year-olds votes in local, state, or national elections; and employers reject 1 of 20 applicants for entry-level jobs because of unlearned work skills.

AmeriCorps and National Service

President Bill Clinton, long an advocate of youth service, initiated the nation's first domestic national service program, named AmeriCorps. At the same time, he initiated programs in service learning throughout the 50 states, allowing each state to determine its own service agenda. AmeriCorps participants receive a small stipend as well as funds reserved for the close of their service period, when they may be used for study in technical institutes as well as colleges and universities.

The service-learning programs are governed by state commissions, often combining school districts with community service organizations. Students today have not only the opportunity to do service while in school but also the freedom to choose civilian or military service, beginning at age 18.

V Is for Value

CITIZENS: MADE NOT BORN

We hold these truths to be self-evident, that all men are created equal, that they are endowed by their Creator with certain unalienable rights, that among these are life, liberty and the pursuit of happiness. That to secure these rights, governments are instituted among men, deriving their just powers from the consent of the governed,—That whenever any form of government becomes destructive of these ends, it is the right of the people to alter or to abolish it, and to institute a new government, laying its foundation on such principles and organizing its powers in such form, as to them shall seem most likely to effect their safety and happiness.

—Thomas Jefferson et al.

Values and choices: desirability, usefulness, importance.

The loudspeaker crackled, interrupting the interdisciplinary history-English class.

"We're delighted to announce that we have been able to secure for today a film that teaches an important value lesson—that we all really are 'created equal,' and that we must not allow ourselves to display or to be the victims of prejudice."

The announcement continued, explaining the place and hours when the film could be viewed. Then a stern voice admonished, "No students remanded to study hall may be excused to see the film."

I burst out laughing—I, the visiting speaker for the 2-hour class session.

The film, titled *Brown Eyes; Blue Eyes,* starts by showing how a teacher treats all those students in her class with brown eyes after she has been told that educational psychologists have determined that all persons with brown eyes are inferior in intellectual ability to those with blue eyes. Halfway through the school year, the same teacher is told that she was given the wrong information; it is the other way around—brown-eyed persons are superior in intellect to those with blue eyes. The camera remains in the classroom, recording how the teacher then changes her treatment of brown-eyed children vis-à-vis blue-eyed children.

Because the film does not contain actors and actresses but faithfully records dramatic behavior and value changes in the treatment of real children in a real classroom, based on grounds so superficial as eye coloring, its message is very powerful.

And here was a school administration, proud of securing the film yet denying its message to the students most in need of learning its lesson. You will not be surprised to know that the school ranks all students by grade level and makes that information public. Nor, I'm sure, will you be surprised to hear that all students are tracked by ability groups, with awards and favors parceled out in descending order.

Nor will you be surprised to learn that community service is a once-a-year, half-day project, with students being delivered to care agencies for a few hours of "volunteer service," followed by essays written during English composition class under the title, "What My Service Meant to Me."

I hope this book makes clear that's not the service learning I am recommending. Those aren't the values I would espouse, nor the choices I would make. Values, though, are being taught—and learned—regardless of whether service learning is part of every student's school experience.

W Is for Who

CITIZENS: MADE NOT BORN

After all, democracy doesn't begin with elections. As events in Eastern Europe have demonstrated, citizen forums precede elections. Dialogue takes place among people who live with the issues day by day. In such dialogues fundamental values emerge. And it is on these values, not who's running for office or the way a particular bill is worded, that they make decisions.

Millions of people across the globe have made the choice for democracy. Now, like us . . . they must begin making the thousands of daily choices about what kind of democracy they will have.

—David Mathews

W is for who is in charge of service learning at school? Of course, that question becomes moot when and if service learning is a natural method of instruction throughout the grades and employed as a teaching strategy in all disciplines. Most schools, though, may wish to have a school-work site coordinator, someone to integrate the school schedule with local job calendars. No reason this could not be

80

done by an adult volunteer, for example, a local retired teacher receiving a modest stipend for handling this assignment.

But you are reading this book because you want to get started or you want to expand your student volunteer activities. Let me suggest three other "whos" that will allow you to get started immediately.

The Social Studies Department

Treating service learning as citizenship education and including civic activity within the teaching of civics from Grade 1 through advanced-placement history courses in senior high school, each school district could make its high school Social Studies Department the coordinating agency for all student community service, perhaps by using adult community volunteers to help with placement and supervision or by using teachers-in-training or college interns as clerks and coordinators.

The Guidance Department

Here is a logical place for coordination, particularly if the guidance department is giving equal attention to those students not going on to postsecondary schooling. If so, then guidance personnel will include men and women knowledgeable about local employment opportunities in commercial, nonprofit, and government offices. With the aid of adult volunteers and college interns, the guidance office could handle the added responsibility of coordinating the school's service activities. Perhaps they could get a retired guidance counselor to volunteer.

This is what happened in one Vermont town. A former work-study administrator who served at the college level agreed to be at the high school a few hours each week, helping interested student volunteers find community service placements.

Before she began showing up in the school cafeteria, none of the high school students held volunteer positions in the community; within 6 months, some 400 students were active as community volunteers.

The Office of the Dean of Students

That is, whoever handles discipline for a school. Maybe there are several such persons; in small schools, it's probably the principal. But again, this is a natural location for a coordinating activity with those local businesses seeking volunteer help. And again, there is no reason this office couldn't be staffed by adult volunteers and college interns.

X Is for Xenophilia

CITIZENS: MADE NOT BORN

Geese, as we all know, fly in a V-like formation. Scientists, studying the flight patterns and behaviors of geese, have learned that as each goose flaps its wings, it creates an uplift for the bird following behind it and just a little to one side. Scientists estimate that flying in this formation, geese add some 70% greater flying range than if each goose flew on its own.

Hence: People who share a common direction and sense of community can get where they are going more quickly and more easily because they are traveling on the thrust of each other.

If a goose falls out of formation, it immediately feels the drag and resistance and gets quickly back into formation to take advantage of the lifting power of the bird in front.

Hence: If we have the sense of a goose, we'll stay in formation with those who are headed in the same direction we are.

When the lead goose is tired, it rotates back and another goose flies point.

Hence: It pays to take turns doing hard jobs.

Scientists have determined that the reason the geese in the rear honk is both to encourage the geese up front and to let them know where the tail end of the formation is.

Hence: We need to be careful when and at whom we honk.

When a goose is sick or wounded and goes down to the ground, two geese pull out of the formation and join the one in trouble, staying until it

is well enough to fly or until it is dead. Then the two (or three) go forward
on their own until they find and join another formation.
Hence: If we have the sense of a goose, we'll stand by each other just like
that.

—Cynthia Parsons

Xenophilia: attraction to or admiration of anything foreign or
strange.

The opposite, of course, is attraction to the status quo.

It's not our children who are afraid of what's foreign or strange.
They are eager explorers of the unknown. The high schoolers who
are partnering severely retarded youngsters see right through the
externals, and all who have watched the interaction remark on how
the partnership improves both.

Children who visit hospice and hospital patients reach out to the
residents with such innocence and love that the patients not only
respond in kind but also begin to see themselves in a more positive
light.

Teens who invite senior citizens to share in a prom love both
teaching and learning different dance steps. But thousands of schoolteachers are textbook bound. They not only want every student to
have the same text and to be using it at the same moment but need
an annotated text for themselves that doesn't just provide test answers but also suggests teaching activities.

For example, they do not readily see how they could teach math
by guiding their students in the creating of graphs for the humane
society, helping with bookkeeping chores at the town hall, assisting
with the inventory in the school supply closet, and so forth.

Thousands of school principals, who believe in purchasing text-book and workbook series and demanding that a certain amount of time be spent each day doing the prescribed exercises, are likely to think that using pen pal activities to teach reading and writing lessons is a very poor substitute for filling in workbook blanks.

In some cases, principals feel sure that although the teachers can handle workbook activity, they know too little of their subject matter to be able to turn service activities into service-learning activities—at least without a script.

If a French teacher, for example, is not really fluent in the language and is dependent on texts and commercial materials, then suggesting that the teacher have students form pen pal relationships with native French speakers, translating all letters into both French and English for homework assignments, might not seem wise. Yet having such a teacher is not wise. And keeping youngsters from interaction with adult speakers of the language they are attempting to learn is even less wise.

There are good teachers in every community. One may be a garage mechanic, another a store clerk, another a retiree who loves poetry, another a former teacher now raising a family, another a business entrepreneur, and another an innkeeper. They should have the opportunity to be the "foreigner" and the "stranger" for the community's children, sharing their knowledge and love of learning with them.

Y Is for Youth

Youth is a passage, a transition period between childhood and adulthood. In the United States, we have prolonged adolescence, or the period of youth, far more than any other society on planet Earth. It is not fair to our youths to keep them dependent, to delay their maturity, and to provide them with the rights of citizenship but shield them from its responsibilities.

True, when we were primarily an agrarian society, even young children were given serious responsibilities and learned early to make life-and-death decisions relating to the safety of animals under their care as well as that of the land, the farm buildings, and all living there.

One way we can help speed the transition for our youths is to provide them with opportunities to exercise serious responsibility. I don't mean that we adults should abandon our own responsibility to guide and support our youths but that we should give them an opportunity to suggest how all of us might do things better. We should listen to them, consider their suggestions, and together decide what course of action is best.

Learning From Our Children

In this matter of community service, we might well learn from our children what needs to be done and how to set about doing it.

For example, a youngster volunteered to play Bingo with a blind resident of a nursing home. When the youngster climbed the stairs to the third floor, her destination, her sensitive nose noticed that the odors on the second floor were more pleasant than those on the third. She asked the first nurse she came to what the difference was between residents on those floors and learned that those on the third had their bills paid out of public funds, but those on the second paid their own bills. She asked if those on the second paid more than those on the third and learned that the fees were essentially comparable.

After helping her new friend at Bingo (they won several games), she went to the director's office and told him that she knew he did not keep the third floor as clean as the second, because the people on the third floor didn't have "important" visitors but that she was important and that she was coming back the next week and . . .

This high schooler did not stop until services for the public patients improved dramatically.

Listening to Our Children

The conference was all about "valuing youth." We were there to learn how youngsters struggling with academics in junior high tutored children with learning problems in the elementary grades, which helped improve reading scores for all involved.

I had been assigned two youngsters. The boy explained that he was a gofer for the third grade teacher and that he wished she would let him read aloud with one of the little boys in her class who was so far behind. The girl explained that she was already a mother (at 14) and that she was teaching a second grader to read, which had helped her spelling and her reading, and that she'd gotten her first library card. And, yes, she was reading to her baby, who was only 4 months old.

Then it was time for questions from those of us who were visiting conferees. One of the visitors asked, "What about the students who do the tutoring; do they feel exploited by the teachers?"

First the superintendent spoke, then the high school principal, then the elementary school principal, then the program's coordinator, and then the third grade teacher. Not one of the adults gave a student the opportunity to answer.

My boy remarked to the two of us, "She asked what we think, maybe they didn't hear that." My girl said, "They heard all right. They don't trust us." My boy, "Yeah, some 'valued youth,' huh!"

Trusting Our Children

Whenever I have the opportunity, I ask service organization supervisors whether the students who volunteer in their agencies ever break their trust, ever deliberately misbehave and cause problems. For example, I have asked countless nursing home administrators if students assigned to help a restricted patient eat a meal have ever been known to yell at the patient, hit the patient, throw the food around, disturb other eaters, or deliberately make trouble.

So far, not one supervisor who has overseen the work of a student volunteer has complained of broken trust or destructive behavior. On the other hand, I have often been told of unacceptable behavior by students whose community service work is mandatory. Yes, responsible behavior comes from who choose to serve; irresponsible behavior from those forced to serve.

Z Is for Zeal

CITIZENS: MADE NOT BORN

It is imperative that we educate coming generations of students to grasp and appreciate their own cultural heritages—to be open and knowledgeable about cultures other than their own—to develop a firm moral base and a strong sense of social responsibility and equality among people.

As educated individuals shaping our society, our momentous responsibility is that of forging the distinction between servitude and service. For, thanks to the good fortune of our history and the sacrifices of our predecessors, we enjoy the freedom to reject servitude in its many forms. But our privilege in this regard and our great intellectual legacy mean that we are far from free to ignore the summons to service. Indeed, no claim upon our lives is greater.

Freed from servitude, our lives are freed for service.

—Michele Tolela Myers

We make a living by what we get, but we make a life by what we give.

—*Winston Churchill*

Useful Resources:
Books and Reports

Angelis, J. (1990). *Intergenerational service-learning: Strategies for the future.* Carbondale: Illinois Intergenerational Initiative.

Bartlett, J. (1980). *Familiar quotations* (15th ed.). Boston: Little, Brown.

Constitutional Rights Foundation. *Bill of rights in action* [Newsletter]. Los Angeles: Author.

Gardner, J. W. (1990). *On leadership.* New York: Free Press.

Harrison, C. H. (1987). *Student service.* Princeton, NJ: Carnegie Foundation for the Advancement of Teaching.

Jervis, K., & Tobier, A. (Eds.). (1988). *Education for democracy. Proceedings from the Cambridge school conference on progressive education, October 1987.* Weston, MA: Cambridge School.

Kershner, F., Jr. (Ed.). (1983). *Tocqueville's America: The great quotations.* Athens: Ohio University Press.

Kingston, R. J. (Ed.). (1985, Fall; 1989, Fall; 1990, Summer). *Kettering Review.* Dayton, OH: Kettering Foundation.

La Raus, R., & Remy, R. C. (1978). *Citizenship decision-making.* Menlo Park, CA: Addison-Wesley.

Latham E. (Ed.). (1976). *The declaration of independence and the constitution.* Lexington, MA: D. C. Heath.

Martz, L. (1992). *Making schools better*. New York: Times Books.

Mehlinger, H. D. (1981). *Teaching about the constitution*. Washington, DC: American Historical Association.

Meyer, S. M., Jr. (1989). Youth and service: Why? In Edwin Gould Foundation for Children (Ed.), *Making small "d" democrats: A statement on community service* (pp. 1-6). New York: Editor.

Nathan, J. (1983). *Free to teach: Achieving equity and excellence in schools*. New York: Pilgrim Press.

National Science Foundation. (1991). *Assessing student learning*. Washington, DC: Author.

Network Hotline. The federal Commission on National and Community Service has given a grant to the Minnesota-based NYLC to maintain a hotline for information about and source material for service learning. The number is 1-800-808-7378.

O'Neill, J. (1990). *Changing perspectives: Youth as resources*. Washington, DC: National Crime Prevention Council.

Parsons, C. (1985). *Seeds: Some good ways to improve our schools*. Santa Barbara, CA: Woodbridge.

Parsons, C. (1991). *The co-op bridge*. Santa Barbara, CA: Woodbridge.

People for the American Way. (1989). *Democracy's next generation*. Washington, DC: Author.

Remy, R. C. (1980). *Handbook of basic citizenship competencies*. Alexandria, VA: Association for Supervision and Curriculum Development.

Turner, M. J. (1980). *A guide to basic citizenship competencies*. Columbus: Ohio State University Press.

Welch, W. (1981). *The art of political thinking*. Totowa, NJ: Littlefield, Adams.

CORWIN
PRESS

The Corwin Press logo—a raven striding across an open book—represents the happy union of courage and learning. We are a professional-level publisher of books and journals for K-12 educators, and we are committed to creating and providing resources that embody these qualities. Corwin's motto is "Success for All Learners."